Connecting and Perceiving: The Future of Wireless Networks

Ravi

Contents

Chapter 1

Introduction

This chapter serves as an introductory overview of the book. Section 1.1 introduces the background for Joint Communication and Sensing (JCAS), including its conceptual evolution and technological significance. This section outlines the framework of Perceptive Mobile Networks (PMN) and discusses the sensing functionalities enabled by this architecture. Additionally, it offers a concise introduction to some wireless technologies applied for localization. Section 1.2 presents an overview of the research contents, including the motivations and objectives of this research. It also underlines the challenges in this research and the research methodology to address them. Section 1.3 summarizes the major contributions of this research. Section 1.4 offers the organizational structure of the book.

1.1 Background

1.1.1 Concept of Joint Communication and Sensing

For decades, contemporary wireless communication and radar technology have been developing "in parallel with limited intersections" [1]. However, the increasingly scarce spectrum becomes overwhelmingly congested due to the proliferation of diverse wireless applications. Spectral congestion raises concerns over electromagnetic compatibility in some scenarios. In the early periods, proposed solutions evolved from RF isolation and co-existence to subsequent RF cooperation [2]. Intriguingly, wireless communication and radar systems share analogous hardware components and signal-processing units. Thus, it emerges as a logical proposition to develop an integrated system with both communication and radar sensing functionalities by sharing a transmitting waveform and a majority of hardware modules. This intuitive idea has evolved over the past decade into what is now termed Joint Communication and Sensing (JCAS), or Integrated Sensing and Communication (ISAC) [3], [4]. This promising architecture not only boosts spectrum efficiency by mitigating mutual interference but also reduces energy consumption and implementation costs.

1.1.2 Framework and Sensing Functionalities of the Perceptive Mobile Networks

Implementing the JCAS philosophy in large-scale cellular networks promises to revolutionize the existing cellular mobile networks to the Perceptive Mobile Networks (PMN) [1], [5]. Figure 1.1 in [5] envisages the framework of the PMN and illustrates the general mechanisms of sensing. In a mobile network, numerous base stations (BS), fixed wireless access points (FWA) and user equipment (UE) work similarly to mono-static and bi-static radar setups. RF Remote Radio Units (RRU) are clock-synchronized through a time-allocation mechanism. Signal processing and sensing modules are embedded in a central node that includes Baseband Units (BBU), which have high calculation capacity. Under these circumstances, the locations of all RRUs are fixed, and the positions of

FWAs and UE are also pre-determined.

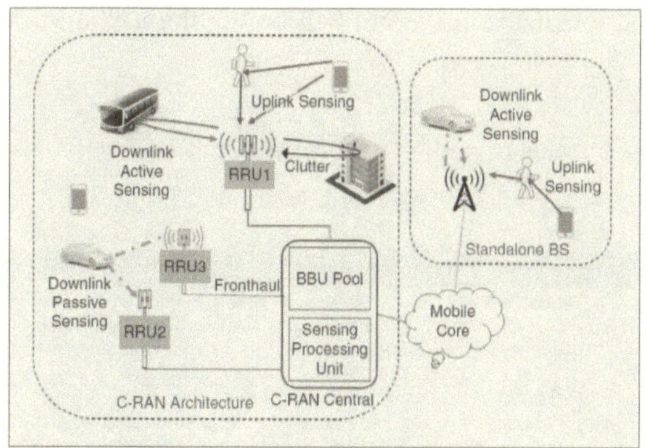

Figure 1.1: Framework of the Perceptive Mobile Networks [5]

The PMN encompasses three categories of sensing mechanisms [1]. The first category is downlink active sensing (DLAS), where an RRU works similarly to a mono-static radar. It captures its own transmitted signals and senses distant targets. DLAS entails in-band full-duplex operation to avoid RF leakage from transmitters. However, this technique is currently immature in practical applications. The second type is downlink passive sensing (DLPS). Analogous to a bi-static/multi-static setup, an RRU receives reflected signals transmitted by other cooperative RRUs. Nevertheless, DLPS requires strict time-synchronization among RRUs. The third category is uplink sensing (ULS), where an RRU perceives the ambience with reflected signals from UE or FWAs. Notably, ULS requires the fewest system architectural adaptations and thus attracts considerable research attention. However, in an uplink setup, clock asynchrony between the transmitters (TXs) and receivers (RXs) incurs time-variant phase shifts and results in estimation ambiguity [6]. The existing solutions to this issue include the use of a "global reference clock, single-node-based and network-based solutions" [7]. Table 1.1 summarizes the classification and technical issues related to these solutions [7]. In this work, CACC-based and CSIR-based schemes for a single-node-based localization system will be highlighted and reviewed in detail in Chapter 2.

Table 1.1: Classification of existing solutions to the clock asynchronism problem [7]

Techniques		Merits	Issues
Using global reference clock	GPS disciplined	Low-cost hardware-based implementation; no additional signal processing complexity.	Require satellite visibility and be constrained to outdoor applications; Solutions that well balance synchronization speed and accuracy are yet to be developed.
	GPS-aided time stamping		
Single node based	Cross-antenna cross-correlation	Exploit locked-clock across multiple receiving channels; Easy to implement without requiring changes to current network and hardware infrastructure.	Require multiple receiving channels; Constrained applications due to algorithm requirements, capability, and complexity
	Cross-antenna signal ratio		
Network based.	Deterministic methods	Explore strength of networked nodes; Improved sensing capability with "multiview" and signal diversity.	Significantly increased complexity and information exchange overhead.
	Stochastic methods		

1.1.3 Human Motion Detection and Localization Based on Wireless Infrastructure

The PMN technology will initiate a variety of emerging sensing applications, such as high-accuracy localization and tracking, human activity recognition, environmental sensing, and sensing-assisted communication, just to name a few. One of the applications is indoor human motion detection and localization via ubiquitous wireless infrastructure. From a device perspective [8], wireless indoor localization systems are classified into device-based and device-free. Device-based localization is the case in which the targets carry user devices, such as smartphones or tablets etc. Therefore, localization is realized through information exchanges between user devices and anchor points. Signal processing, in this scenario, is conducted by a central server. Generally speaking, device-based localization is employed to track cooperative targets that deliberately carry wireless devices to be positioned. Typical use cases include location-based customer service, indoor navigation, home care etc. By contrast, device-free localization, also known as passive localization, is the case in which targets do not carry user devices. Therefore, localization is performed by utilizing the targets' impacts on wireless channels. In comparison, device-free systems and technologies find broader applications, especially in scenarios including security surveillance and emergency rescue where user devices may not be attached to human targets.

Varieties of existing wireless technologies are employed in both device-based and device-free applications. Considering the ubiquity of infrastructure, the most widely implemented wireless indoor positioning systems rely on Wi-Fi, cellular networks, Bluetooth and LoRa technology. With ubiquitous infrastructure and availability on personal smartphones, Wi-Fi-based localization is the most extensively studied field. A large body of Wi-Fi-based systems utilize diverse tracking techniques. Compared with early technologies, recent Wi-Fi localization systems work in a MIMO setup. SpotFi [9] represents a typical device-based localization solution employing 3 Wi-Fi links, achieving a median tracking accuracy of 0.4 meters. On the other hand, Widar 2.0 [10], a device-free tracking system utilizing a single Wi-Fi link, realizes a comparable median accuracy of 0.75 meters. Bluetooth, widely available on smartphones, has also been developed for short-range tracking [11]. For example, Apple's iBeacon adopts an inquiry-based positioning approach, leveraging Received Signal Strength (RSS) measurements. However, Bluetooth's inherent short-range coverage limits its capability and is confined to proximity sensing. LoRa, an industrial IoT technology, utilizes a chirp spread spectrum modulation technique and is less susceptible to indoor multi-path effects. Experiments [12] demonstrate that a LoRa indoor localization system utilizing an RSSI-based fingerprint method achieves a mean error of 2.2 m in the 2.4 GHz band. However, the availability of LoRa is still confined to specific scenarios, hindering it from ubiquitous deployment. Compared with Wi-Fi-based systems, cellular networks provide seamless integration for indoor and outdoor scenarios, highlighting its potential in both outdoor and indoor localization. In [13], passive localization with meter-level precision is implemented through the channel estimation of LTE signals. Moreover, the dense deployment of small cells in office buildings will enable better tracking performance with a networked sensing capability shortly.

1.2 Research Contents

1.2.1 Motivations

Currently, there has been extensive research on device-free human localization techniques based on Wi-Fi technology, whereas there are relatively fewer reports on localization algorithms and real-time systems using cellular mobile networks. As the PMN promises a vision for broad applications in the next-generation mobile networks, this **book** aims to develop a real-time localization demonstrator using uplink LTE-based signals.

1.2.2 Objectives

- *Objective 1*

    To design a human motion detection and tracking scheme employing the MIMO setup and LTE-based signal structure

Clock asynchrony in ULS setup introduces unknown and slowly time-varying phase shifts in CSI samples. By leveraging the MIMO setup and a related signal model, this **book** aims to design a scheme to estimate Doppler frequency, angle-of-arrival (AoA) and propagation delay with real-time capability.

- *Objective 2*

  To develop and implement a real-time human motion detection and localization demonstrator for an LTE-based JCAS system.

By leveraging the National Instrument (NI) Massive MIMO prototyping system
as the development platform, this work aims to implement a real-time human localization demonstrator. It is enabled by designing a customized CSI-streaming
interface and implementing the tracking scheme specified in *Objective 1*.

1.2.3   Challenges

- *Challenges 1*

  The LTE signal structure contains 100 subcarriers for a single spatial layer,
  leading to more intensive computations than Wi-Fi-based implementations.

Compliant with the 3GPP LTE standard [14], an LTE pilot symbol is modulated
with 1200 valid subcarriers. In this demonstrator, only one single spatial layer
is activated for transmission. As a result, the test bed employs 100 active pilots,
more than triple the subcarriers in a Wi-Fi-based system. The increase in the
number of subcarriers leads to higher computational complexity and poses more
challenges to real-time implementation.

- *Challenges 2*

  Unlike the availability of well-developed CSI-reading tools in Wi-Fi-based
  applications, there are no existing software packages available to extract
  CSI samples from the LTE-based commercial prototyping platform.

Extensive studies on Wi-Fi-based are performed utilising well-developed CSI-extracting tools to acquire CSI data from off-the-shelf network interface cards (NIC) like Atheors 9580 and Intel 5300. On the contrary, to the best of my knowledge, there are no existing software packages available to read CSI samples from the NI Massive MIMO prototyping system. Therefore, a customized CSI-streaming interface compatible with the development platform needs to be developed.

1.2.4 Research Methodology

Based on the literature review in Chapter 2, in the single-node-based scenario, CACC-based and CSIR-based methods are potential candidates for the elimination of random phase shifts. A well-structured motion detection and localization scheme will be designed that incorporates the advantages of these techniques and best matches the LTE signal characteristics. Implemented on an existing LTE-based software-defined radio platform, this work will design a customized CSI-reading module tailored for real-time localization.

1.3   Research Contributions

- *Contributions 1*

  This book proposes an effective tracking scheme that integrates a CSIR-based Doppler frequency estimator with a maximum likelihood estimation-based (MLE-based) estimator for AoA and delay estimation.

This book proposes a tracking scheme that combines a CSIR-based Doppler frequency estimator and an MLE-based estimator for AoA and delay estimation. The CSIR-based Doppler frequency estimator is based on a refined Mobius transformation approach in [15], which enables estimating robust Doppler frequency with noisy signal samples and features less computational complexity with increased subcarriers. Through CSI self-correlation, the random phase shifts in received signals are eliminated. The MLE-based approach enables the AoA and propagation delay to be estimated by aggregating CSI samples from successive sampling windows. To ensure robust motion detection and handle system anomalies, this scheme also incorporates a motion confirmation process to mitigate false detection. Evaluations show that the proposed tracking scheme achieves sub-meter tracking accuracy with uncompromising real-time capability.

- *Contributions 2*

  A real-time human motion detection and tracking demonstration test bed using LTE signals has been successfully designed and implemented.

This work designs and implements a customized pilot-streaming interface, which prepares and streams active pilot samples to the UDP port. In the meantime, a target-tracking module is developed in Python, which simultaneously reads pilots from a UDP port, performs target-tracking within a sampling window, and displays updated positions on the monitor. By intricately synchronizing the two modules, a real-time human motion detection and tracking demonstration test bed has been successfully implemented and evaluated to achieve sub-meter localization accuracy.

1.4   Organization of the book

The rest of the book is organized as follows. Chapter 2 presents the literature review on human motion detection and tracking using wireless communication technologies.

Chapter 3 proposes the detection and tracking scheme. Section 3.2 presents the workflow of this demonstrator. Section 3.3 introduces the CSI ratio-based (CSIR-based) Doppler frequency estimator and the maximum likelihood-based (MLE-based) AoA and delay estimators. Section 3.4 examines the selection of parameters for signal processing.

Chapter 4 details the design and implementation of this motion detection and tracking demonstration system. Section 4.2 presents the overview of this demonstrator, including the system setup and its operational procedures. Section 4.3 introduces the signal structure employed in this demonstrator. Section 4.4 elaborates on the development of the pilot-streaming interface. Section 4.5 specifies the software implementation of the target-tracking module.

Chapter 5 details the experimental evaluations of this demonstration test bed, aiming to thoroughly assess the system's tracking performance and validate its suitability in real-world scenarios. Sec 5.2 provides an overview of the experimental implementation, testing methodology, as well as data processing and visualization techniques. Sec 5.3 introduces the calibration procedure for transceiver channels. Sec 5.4 presents the impact of UE locations on the localization performance and thereafter determines an optimized UE location for the following evaluations. Sec 5.5 reveals the impact of walking speed on tracking. Sec 5.6 extends the application of the system to non-line-of-sight (NLoS) scenarios.

Chapter 6 reviews the main contributions of the **book** and looks forward to our future work.

Chapter 2

Literature Review

2.1 Introduction

This chapter provides a comprehensive review of the existing techniques and methodologies utilized for wireless human localization, with a specific focus on localization within the uplink sensing (ULS) setup. Section 2.2 introduces the signal metrics employed in indoor localization for both device-based and device-free applications. Section 2.3 reviews the localization schemes and implementations based on Channel State Information. The model-based approaches are highlighted while pattern-based methods are also briefly covered. Section 2.4 offers a concise summary of the chapter's contents.

2.2 Signal Metrics and Techniques for Indoor Human Localization

Depending on whether localization is device-based or device-free, various techniques are available, each working on distinct signal metrics. Figure 2.1 illustrates the taxonomy of these techniques [8], [16]. The primary signal metrics include Received Signal Strength (RSS), Channel State Information (CSI), Angle of Arrival (AoA), Time of Arrival (ToA) and Time Difference of Arrival (TDoA). These metrics can be utilized either independently or jointly for positioning.

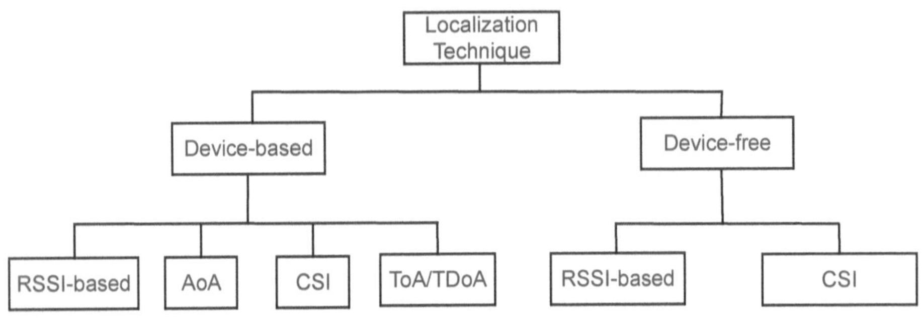

Figure 2.1: Taxonomy of indoor localization techniques

2.2.1 Received Signal Strength Indicator

Received Signal Strength (RSS) is the actual signal power strength measured at a receiver. On the other hand, Received Signal Strength Indicator (RSSI), is a normalized value of RSS, and is almost arbitrarily defined by any chip vendor [11], [17]. This implies that identical RSS values collected by Wi-Fi network interface cards (NIC) from different suppliers may be mapped to different RSSI values. Nevertheless, variations in RSS or RSSI are of main interest for localization. In a multi-path environment, the RSSI value is inversely proportional to the distance between a transmitter (TX) and a receiver (RX), as represented in Equation (2.1). In (2.1), d is the TX-to-RX distance, and $RSSI_0$ is the RSSI value at a reference point (RP). The path loss exponent, α, typically between 2 and 4 in an indoor environment [11], can be theoretically determined through curve fitting based on RSSI measurements in a specific environment. In device-based scenarios, the RSSI-based approach is employed to localize a user node through trilateration or multilateration. Figure 2.2 illustrates the principles of trilateration. In practice, multilateration is favoured for its improved accuracy, as it exhibits greater tolerance to fluctuations in RSSI values.

$$\text{RSSI} = -n10log_n\left(d\right) + \text{RSSI}_0 \qquad (2.1)$$

[Production note: This figure is not included in this digital copy due to copyright restrictions.]

Figure 2.2: Principle of trilateration [11]

However, traditional RSSI-based localization systems achieve a median accuracy range of 2 to 4 meters [9], and this relatively lower accuracy is attributed to severe temporal fluctuations of RSSI. According to [18], the RSSI variations at a stationary receiver may reach as large as 5 dB in one minute in laboratory environments. Since RSSI represents the superimposition of multipath signals, it fails to distinguish the multi-path effect on individual spectral components. In this context, RSSI is considered a coarsely-grained metric for indoor positioning. To address this challenge, fingerprint-based solutions have been developed to improve accuracy by making a complete radio map with finer granularity in the areas of interest. Fingerprint-based schemes generally comprise an offline stage and an online stage [17]. In the offline stage, a comprehensive radio map is constructed to collect RSSI values at every RP within the area of interest. In the online stage, the algorithm compares the actual RSSI measurements with the radio fingerprinting map to estimate positions accurately. Furthermore, the state-of-art technology in this area integrates fingerprinting with deep-learning methods. RSSI-based indoor localization via deep-learning methods necessitates high-quality radio maps and specialized algorithms. A wide array of data pre-processing approaches, such as data augmentation techniques and learning models, have been proposed to improve the robustness and accuracy of fingerprinting [19].

2.2.2   Channel State Information

The channel frequency response (CFR) characterizes the signal propagation behaviour between a TX and a RX in the frequency domain. Compared with RSSI, CFR is a finer-grained metric that features subcarrier-level resolution to distinguish the effect of frequency-selective fading on each subcarrier component. In a typical MIMO-OFDM system, the CFRs characterizing each TX-RX channel are collectively represented in a matrix form called Channel State Information (CSI). The CSI matrix at any time instance is a 3D complex matrix, with each entry represented in Equation (2.2) [20].

$$[\text{Production note: This equation is not included in this digital copy due to copyright restrictions.}] \tag{2.2}$$

where,

a_n : complex amplitude of the baseband received signal along the n_{th} propagation path

$d_{i,j,n}$: path length from the i_{th} transmit antenna to the j_{th} receive antenna of the n_{th} path

f_k : k_{th} subcarrier frequency

τ_i : the time delay from Cyclic Shift Diversity of the i_{th} transmit antenna

ρ : the Sampling Time Offset

η : the Sampling Frequency Offset

$q_{i,j}$, $\zeta_{i,j}$: amplitude attenuation and phase shift of the (i, j) element beamforming matrix

This equation accounts for both multi-path channel effects and the clock asynchrony between the TX and the RX. Furthermore, the time sequence of CSI matrices records the variations of the wireless propagation channel. A comparison between RSSI and CSI is listed in Table 2.1 [21], demonstrating that CSI data feature more information and stability. Therefore, CSI provides fine-grained solutions for more complicated sensing problems. Nevertheless, CSI is not as readily available as RSSI. CSI is currently only accessible to some CSI tools, accompanied by specific Wi-Fi NICs [21]. Given its significance in wireless indoor localization, CSI-based indoor localization will be closely studied in detail in Section 2.3.

Table 2.1: Comparison between RSSI and CSI [21]

Metric	RSSI	CSI
Network layer	MAC layer	Physical layer
Time resolution	Packet size	Multipath signal cluster scale
Frequency resolution	No	Subcarrier scale
Temporal stability	Low	High
Measurement band	RF band	Base band
Granularity	Coarse-grained (per packet)	Fine-grained (per subcarrier)
Universality	Almost all Wi-Fi devices	Some Wi-Fi devices

2.2.3 Angle of Arrival

In a MIMO configuration, an antenna array is utilized to estimate the incident angle of received signals at the access point's (AP) receivers. Once the AoAs at two APs are determined, the user device can be readily located by a triangulation method. However, the performance of AoA estimation is susceptible to multi-path effects and non-line-of-sight (NLoS) conditions [11]. Multiple Signal Classification (MUSIC) algorithms are commonly used to achieve a finer angle resolution with an antenna array of limited antenna elements. ArrayTrack [22] utilizes a 16-element array for each AP to obtain precise AoA estimates and attains a median accuracy of 23 cm. It combines independent AoA estimates from the antenna pairs and identifies the direct line-of-sight (LoS) component whose phases appear stabler across consecutive samples. However, the use of specialized hardware and collaborative measurements by multiple APs is infeasible with commodity-of-the-shelf (COTS) devices.

2.2.4 Time of Arrival and Time Difference of Arrival

Temporal parameters such as ToA or TDoA are exploited primarily in device-based applications. ToA is the absolute signal propagation time from a TX to a RX. Should the exact ToA be estimated, the distance would be simply calculated by multiplying ToA and the light speed. However, this necessitates strict clock synchronization between the TX and the RX, making it impractical for most mobile communication infrastructures. For example, timing in Wi-Fi-based systems is acquired by extracting time stamps in the received packages. Wi-Fi signals compliant with 802.11n/ac standards span across 40 MHz, equivalent to 25 nanoseconds per packet. During that time interval, signals travel about 1.9 meters, thus leading to coarse range resolution [23]. Chronos emulates a wideband system by hopping between multiple Wi-Fi bands to obtain sub-nanosecond ToA [24]. Moreover, it identifies the direct path with the minimum phase shifts. As a result, Chronos leverages one AP to achieve a median localization accuracy of 65 cm in LoS scenarios and 98 cm in NLoS scenarios. However, the techniques used by Chronos can not be generalized since it is not built on community Wi-Fi devices.

On the other hand, some indoor localization systems leverage TDoA-based approaches. These methods involve measuring the time difference it takes for signals to travel from two anchor nodes to the user device. Consequently, a user device is located along a hyperbola with the two anchor nodes as its foci. With at least three anchor nodes, the user device can be located where the three hyperbolas meet. One such system, Tonetrack is developed on the Wireless Open Access Research Platform (WARP) [25]. It achieves a median accuracy of 0.9 meters with a 20 MHz bandwidth. Similar to Chronos, it aggregates multiple frequency-hopping channels to simulate a broader bandwidth. Unfortunately, this technique is not deployable with COTS devices either. Although neither ToA nor TDoA can be precisely acquired from COTS devices, these coarse-grained parameters serve as indicators for the direct path and can be exploited for joint parameter estimation. [9], [10].

2.3 CSI-based Indoor Localization Approaches and Systems

Compared with RSSI and other signal metrics, CSI provides finer granularity and thus holds more potential for localization and sensing applications. This section reviews various CSI-based indoor localization approaches and systems.

CSI-based sensing methods are roughly categorized into pattern-based methods and model-based methods [26]. Pattern-based methods attempt to establish the relationships between signal variation features and specific human activities. To this end, pattern-based methods extract particular features from a large body of preprocessed data and train a classifier for subsequent recognition. By contrast, model-based methods necessitate purpose-specific models to be established, revealing the quantitative relationships between the sensed parameters and CSI measurements. In most cases, pattern-based methods entail a time-consuming training process and depend on specific settings. Model-based methods, in comparison, achieve better performance and are less dependent on the environment. Whatever methods are chosen, the clock asynchronism-induced phase shifts should be first addressed in the preprocessing phase if the CSI phases are involved in a model.

2.3.1 CSI-based Indoor Human Localization via Model-based Methods

Depending on diverse system setups and physical quantities to be exploited, a couple of CSI models have been developed for human localization [27]. Among these models, AoA models are the most widely utilized, owing to the prevalent deployment of MIMO systems [10], [22] [28]–[32]. In these schemes, the MUSIC algorithm and its variations are utilized to enhance angle resolution. It's important to note that AoA models are applicable only when the receiver antennas are situated within the far-field region of the transmitter antennas.

On the other hand, the Fresnel zone model [33], [34] is a recently proposed model grounded in the physical principles of the Fresnel zone. This model correlates signal variations with the target's positions when the target traverses different

Fresnel zones. Notably, both AoA and Fresnel models may incorporate other signal metrics including ToA, TDoA and even RSSI, aiming at higher tracking accuracy [9], [10], [35].

SpotFi [9] is deployed with 4 to 5 COTS APs in a room. The APs work in monitor mode and capture Wi-Fi packets from a smartphone carried by a target. A central server is responsible for collecting and processing the CSI samples. To remove the random phase shifts caused by clock asynchronism, SpotFi employs a linear fitting-based "sanitization" algorithm. This algorithm assumes the presence of linear phase relationships among the random phase shifts across the packets. Moreover, SpotFi significantly improves its multipath disentanglement capability by utilizing measurable phase differences across subcarriers, effectively creating "virtual sensors". Thirdly, assuming that the direct path has the minimum ToA, SpotFi identifies the direct path with the highest likelihood. After identifying a direct path, SpotFi maps the received RSSI to the distance with a well-acknowledged RSSI model and localizes the target. SpotFi attains a median positioning accuracy of 40 cm. However, this scheme is computationally intensive, which hinders SpotFi from real-time implementation.

Widar [36] introduces a mobility model that relies on 6 Wi-Fi links for passive human tracking. This scheme achieves a localization accuracy of 25 cm with an initial position and 38 cm without this knowledge. The mobility model correlates geometrically the CSI data with a target's location and velocity. It extracts the variation rate of each signal propagation path length (termed PLCR in the paper). and estimates both a user's speed and position geometrically. Specifically, PLCR is retrieved through two steps. First, Widar refines the raw CSI data through Principal Component Analysis (PCA) and applies Short-time

Fourier Transformation (STFT) to acquire the complete PLCR spectrogram. Second, Widar decimates the spectrogram in the time domain by setting a threshold on the maximum acceleration of a human walk. Consequently, the optimal PLCR is acquired by solving a dynamic programming problem. Once PLCR is extracted, the velocity is determined and successive positioning is conducted by a simple motion equation. One limitation of Widar is its reliance on a significant number of Wi-Fi links and the need for an initial position for continuous tracking. Additionally, the paper does not claim real-time tracking capabilities for this system.

MaTrack [28] employs the AoA model, and proposes a novel Dynamic-MUSIC method which distinguishes dynamic signals from static signals. Subsequently, MaTrack estimates the incident angle of dynamic signals at two receivers and localizes the target by synchronizing the AoA estimates from all the available receiver pairs. It is reported to achieve a median accuracy of 0.6 meters with only two COTS APs, each assembled with 3 antennas. To refine the conventional MUSIC algorithm and solve the multi-path problem, the scheme utilizes the intuition that static signals are coherent with each other whereas dynamic signals are not. Once the coherence is removed, the dynamic paths are detected. In addition, the scheme also employs a linear fitting method to remove the time-variant phase shifts and align all the associated ToAs across packets, facilitating AoA and ToA estimation. The paper does not report the real-time performance of Matrack.

The AoA model may result in erroneous results when a target obstructs the LOS path, whereas the Fresnel zone model assumes that the targets transverse different Fresnel zones between the transmitter and the receiver.

LiFs [33] and MFDL [34] are localization systems that rely on the Fresnel zone model. LiFs utilizes subcarriers that are not impacted by multi-path reflections in noisy environments. This system achieves a positioning accuracy of 0.5 m in the LoS environment and an accuracy of 1.1 m in the NLoS case. Operating on a power-fading model, the algorithm excludes the subcarriers whose magnitudes rise unexpectedly, contrary to the power-fading model. Localization is conducted by "minimizing the mean absolute distance deviation between the CSI samples and the calculated CSI data" by the physical principles of the Fresnel zone model. By contrast, MFDL formulates a multi-carrier Fresnel penetration model (FPM) to track a walking target with 2 orthogonal receivers. It achieves a median accuracy of 45 cm outdoors and 55 cm indoors. MFDL quantifies the space between a pair of Fresnel zones associated with two subcarriers by calculating the phase difference between the two Fresnel ellipses. This approach allows for the determination of the intersection area between two Fresnel ellipses, enabling the successful positioning of the target, as illustrated in Figure 2.3. The major drawback of the scheme is its reliance on a cumbersome calibration procedure involving a perfect reflector. The paper does not report its real-time performance.

As an updated version of Widar, Widar 2.0 [10] achieves device-free localization with a single Wi-Fi link on COTS devices. Its unified model includes AoA, ToF, and Doppler frequency, devising an efficient algorithm for joint parameter estimation. With real-time capability at a data rate of 250 Hz, Widar 2.0 achieves a median tracking accuracy of 0.75 meters in a tracking area of 6 m × 5 m. Its algorithm manipulates the cross-antenna-cross-correlation (CACC) on CSI data to eliminate the clock asynchrony-induced phase shifts. However, the CACC operation inevitably results in an image Doppler frequency-related component

[Production note: This figure is not included in
this digital copy due to copyright restrictions.]

Figure 2.3: Fresnel zone model [34]

and thus ambiguity in Doppler frequency estimation. The scheme follows the same "add-and-minus" solution in [37]. For simultaneous and joint estimation of multiple parameters, the authors build a unified model based on the maximum likelihood estimation method. Furthermore, it devises a novel graph-based algorithm to distinguish the target's walking trajectories from chaotic multi-path parameters.

WiDFS [38] proposes a lightweight single-target tracking scheme with a single Wi-Fi link. Experimental evaluations demonstrate that WiDFS implements instant positioning with a median positioning deviation of 72 cm in typical indoor environments. To eliminate random phase shifts induced by CFO and TO, CACC and self-correlation operation are utilized in WiDFS's algorithm. Instead of estimating Doppler frequency through the "add-and-minus" method, WiDFS first retrieves the approximate static components by calculating the arithmetic means of CACC results in a sampling window. Consequently, the dynamic components are obtained by simply subtracting the static components from the CACC results. Doppler frequency is deduced with the MUSIC algorithm in every CSI sampling window. In addition, WiDFS utilizes the self-correlation of

CSI to remove random phase shifts caused by clock asynchrony. Subsequently, AoA and propagation delay are respectively estimated by formulating a maximum likelihood problem based on CSI data in a couple of successive sampling windows. WiDFS is capable of real-time human motion tracking at the data rate of 1 KHz, exceeding the performance of Widar 2.0.

Random phase shifts can also be eliminated through the CSI-ratio technique due to the proximity of co-located antennas. Although CSI-ratio has been employed in estimating Doppler frequency in [15], an intricate scheme in [39] is developed to obtain Dopper frequency estimates and fulfil a joint estimation of AoA and delay. Leveraging a truncated Taylor series, the nonlinear CSI ratio representation is converted to a linear function, facilitating the formulation of a MUSIC-type Doppler frequency estimator. The AoA and delay estimates are also acquired with a MUSIC-type algorithm by elaborately assembling the related samples in the spatial domain. The CSIR-based scheme outperforms other benchmarks in scenarios without the existence of a LoS path. However, numerical simulations show that the performance of this scheme degrades when the number of antennas is limited. The paper does not claim its real-time capability.

In summary, CSI-based indoor localization via model-based methods enables sub-meter localization accuracy with good suitability. Some of the localization schemes are promising candidates for real-time positioning implementation.

2.3.2 CSI-based Indoor Localization via Pattern-based Methods

CSI-based indoor localization via pattern-based methods relies on the collection of fingerprints. Currently, CSI amplitude is more widely employed as fingerprints than CSI phase. Therefore, we review some of the pattern-based approaches using CSI amplitude. Before training, raw data must undergo a pre-processing stage to improve the quality of fingerprints. Major preprocessing steps include denoising, selection and classification of data samples, feature refinement, feature retrieval and dimension compression [17]. During training, a few deep learning models are available. For Wi-Fi fingerprints, common deep learning models include Deep Belief Networks (DBNs), Convolutional Neural Networks (CNNs), Generative Adversarial Networks (GANs), Autoencoder (AE) and Recurrent Neural Networks (RNNs) [40].

DeepFi adopts fingerprints of CSI amplitude for indoor localization with a single AP [41]. The scheme allocates a dedicated DBN for each reference point (RP) and refines the parameters using a greedy learning algorithm and reconstruction loss. In the online phase, Bayes' Law is employed to obtain the posterior probability for each RP. The position is estimated by a weighted average of the posterior probabilities at all RPs. Experimental assessments are conducted in LoS and NLoS settings. The localization deviation is 0.94 m in the LoS setting and 1.8 m in the NLoS setting. Notably, the probabilistic calculations result in a large latency in the response time, rendering DeepFi unsuitable for real-time positioning applications.

ConFi undertakes indoor positioning using CSI images and a single AP [42]. To facilitate training via CNNs, CSI-amplitude data are converted into RGB images, termed "CSI images". Additionally, to enhance the efficiency of fingerprint recording, data augmentation is applied to the training process. In the online phase, the system determines the position by calculating a weighted centroid based on the three top-ranking RPs. ConFi achieves a localization accuracy of 1.36 meters, representing a considerable improvement upon DeepFi in the same environment.

A cost-effective approach using GANs to streamline site surveying is proposed in [43]. In the offline phase, A dataset of 5000 CSI amplitude samples is collected at each RP for training, and 100 of them are randomly selected 10,000 times to create amplitude plots across subcarriers. These plots served as input for a GANs model to produce an additional 10,000 plots. The authors employ a Support Vector Machine (SVM) classifier and improve the localization precision. However, a drawback of this method is that a dedicated GAN should be trained for each RP. To mitigate this complexity, they propose using a convolutional GAN (CGAN) to generate fingerprints. This may streamline the process and reduce computational overhead. Performance assessments show that deviations range from 1 to 2 meters.

In summary, the most advanced pattern-based indoor localization systems using CSI fingerprints achieve positioning accuracy ranging from 1 to 2 meters and seem currently incapable of real-time tracking.

2.4 Conclusion

This chapter reviews various indoor localization schemes based on different signal metrics and models. The CSI-based localization methods are reviewed in detail. In the scope of CSI-based positioning schemes, model-based methods outperform pattern-based methods in terms of universality and accuracy. By comparing different device-free localization approaches, it is found that CACC-based and CSIR-based methods are better candidates for both accuracy and real-time performance.

Chapter 3

Human Motion Detection and Tracking Scheme

3.1   Introduction

A real-time human localization system necessitates a robust motion detection workflow and an accurate localization scheme. A robust motion detection procedure is required to identify the system anomalies and mitigate false detection due to signal fluctuations. Additionally, it is also essential to distinguish temporary instances of missing detection from an absence of human movement. Once human motion is confirmed, the system needs to estimate motion-related parameters such as Doppler frequency, angle-of-arrival (AoA), and propagation delay to promptly locate a moving person. This chapter focuses on the motion detection and tracking scheme for the demonstrator, including the workflow, the parameter estimation algorithms and the selection of parameters in the scheme. Section 3.2 presents the workflow of this scheme. Section 3.3 introduces the CSI ratio-based (CSIR-based) Doppler frequency estimator and the maximum likelihood estimation-based (MLE-based) AoA and delay estimators.

Section 3.4 examines the selection of parameters for signal processing. Section 3.5 concludes the work in this chapter.

3.2 Motion Detection and Tracking Workflow

In a real-world radio environment, system anomalies and signal fluctuations may cause instability in a motion-tracking system utilizing a single wireless link. Additionally, wireless signals propagate along complex paths in a multi-path environment, potentially resulting in temporary missing or false detection for certain snapshots. To overcome these challenges, a reliable and resilient workflow is elaborated on in this work, leveraging an iterative procedure to reduce the chances of wrong detection and to handle system exceptions. Figure.3.1

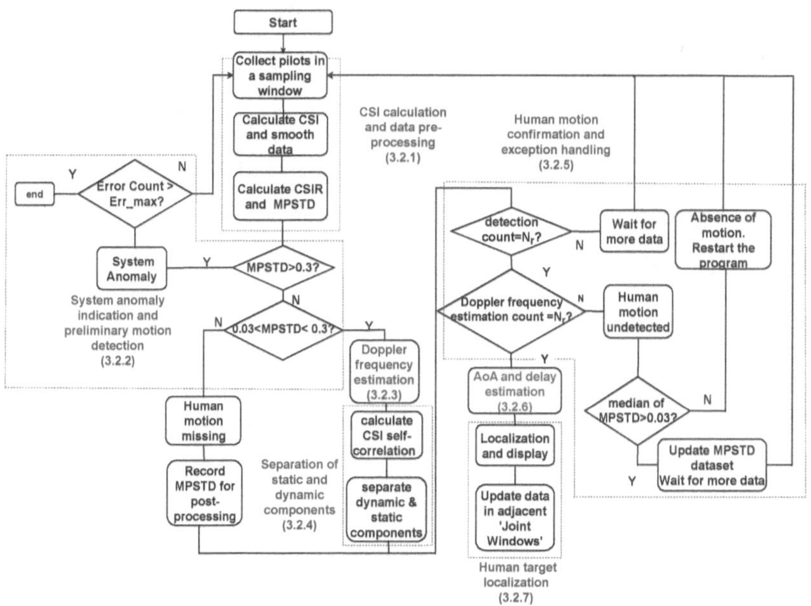

Figure 3.1: Workflow for the motion detection and tracking scheme

illustrates the workflow for the proposed scheme. The major modules include

CSI calculation and data pre-processing, system anomaly indication and preliminary motion detection, Doppler frequency estimation (DFE), separation of static and dynamic components, human motion confirmation and exception handling, AoA and delay estimation, as well as human target localization.

3.2.1 CSI Calculation and Data Pre-processing

This module is responsible for converting received pilots into CSI samples and performing data pre-processing for CSI samples on a "sampling window" basis. A "CSI sampling window" represents a continuous time series during which a collection of CSI samples is processed as once. Typically, a CSI sampling window lasts several hundred milliseconds. The transmitted uplink pilot sequence comprises 1200 randomly generated symbols and is mapped to 12 different user equipment (UE) antennas via orthogonal frequency division multiplexing (OFDM). These received pilots are used for channel estimation in the frequency domain. We define the channel transfer function as H_p, the transmitted pilot symbol at a given subcarrier as x_p, the corresponding received pilot symbol as y_p, and additive Gaussian white noise (AGWN) noise as z_p. As only one UE with a single transmit antenna is employed in this demonstration system, the channel transfer equation is represented in a scalar form as the following.

$$y_p = H_p x_p + z_p \tag{3.1}$$

Multiply (3.1) by x_p^* on both sides and re-order it, and (3.2) follows. Herein, x_p^* is the conjugate of x_p and $x_p x_p^* = \|x_p\|^2 = 1$ for QPSK-modulated pilots.

$$\begin{aligned} H_p &= \frac{y_p x_p^* - z_p x_p^*}{\|x_p x_p^*\|} \\ &= y_p x_p^* - z_p x_p^* \end{aligned} \tag{3.2}$$

As channel estimations are conducted on a sampling window of received symbols, $z_p x_p^*$ can be omitted by being averaged. Then, the channel transfer function estimate, $\tilde{H}_p$, is defined as in (3.3).

$$\tilde{H}_p \approx y_p x_p^* \tag{3.3}$$

To ensure accurate detection and estimation, it is crucial to remove outliers and noise in the raw data. Therefore, a combination of a Savitzky-Golay smoother and a low-pass filter (LPF) is utilized to reject outliers and high-frequency noise. Assumes that a person typically walks at a speed lower than 3.5 meters per second indoors, the maximum Doppler frequency induced by human movement at the centre frequency of 3.1 GHz, is estimated as

$$f_D = \frac{3.5}{3 \times 10^8} \times 3.1 \times 10^9 \, (Hz) \approx 36.17 \, (Hz) \tag{3.4}$$

Thus, a cutting frequency of 50 Hz is chosen for an LPF to filter high-frequency components. Figure.3.2 demonstrates the pre-processing effect on raw CSI samples, and it is evident that the output signals smoothed largely.

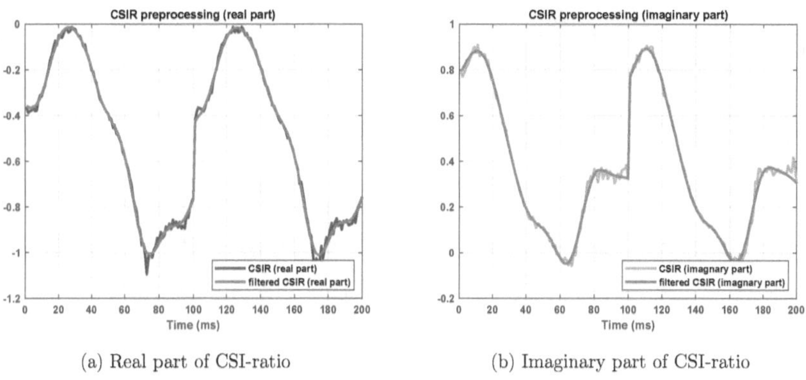

(a) Real part of CSI-ratio

(b) Imaginary part of CSI-ratio

Figure 3.2: Pre-processing for CSI-ratio samples

3.2.2 System Anomaly Indication and Preliminary Motion Detection

This module is responsible for identifying system anomalies and coarsely detecting human motion. Temporary instability or interruptions may occur in real-world communication links. Once this happens, pilot data may be corrupted, potentially leading to unreliable human motion sensing. Hence, criteria are essential to indicate system anomalies, human motion, and static scenarios. Experimental results demonstrate that phases of CSI ratio samples can be utilized as a metric for this purpose. Specifically, phases of CSI ratio samples surge abruptly and irregularly when instability in communication links occurs, whereas they display regular and periodical fluctuations due to human motion. By contrast, this metric exhibits random small variations in static situations. To elaborate this metric with OFDM signals and mitigate the effect of asynchrony, this proposed scheme leverages the median phase standard deviation (MPSTD) of CSI ratio samples across different subcarriers in a sampling window to discriminate system anomalies, human motion and static scenarios.

MPSTD is defined in (3.5). Firstly, the phase standard deviations of CSI ratio samples in a sampling window are calculated for all the subcarriers. Secondly, the median of this collection of phase standard deviations is obtained. Here, σ_j is the phase standard deviation of CSI ratio samples for the j_{th} subcarrier, and φ_{ij} is the phase of the i_{th} CSI ratio sample in a sampling window for the j_{th} subcarrier, and $\bar{\varphi}_j$ is the mean of φ_{ij} in this sampling window.

$$\begin{cases} \sigma_j = \sqrt{\dfrac{\sum_{i=1}^{n} (\varphi_{ij} - \bar{\varphi}_j)^2}{n-1}} \\ MPSTD = Median\{\sigma_1, \sigma_2, ...\sigma_M\} \end{cases} \tag{3.5}$$

Figure 3.3 demonstrates the MPSTD variations in some typical circumstances. Figure 3.3 (a) shows the variations of MPSTD in the cases of system anomaly and human motion. As is illustrated, when a communication link becomes unstable, the MPSTD curve shows impulses, rising dramatically and irregularly. By constant, although human motion induces fluctuations of the MPSTD curve, the variation magnitude is substantially lower. In Figure 3.3 (b), MPSTD curves for human motion and static scenarios are presented with a stable communication link. Specifically, the blue line representing human motion demonstrates periodicity and much larger amplitude than other cases. The amplitude of MPSTD ranges between nearly 0.03 and 0.2. In comparison, in static scenarios where a person stands or sits before the receiver or when the room is vacant, the MPSTD curves show much slighter variations with a magnitude lower than 0.03. As above, it is likely to choose a set of thresholds to classify different scenarios into system anomaly, human motion and static situations. The criteria are summarized in (3.6). Moreover, in this demonstration test bed, if system anomalies persist for specified times, the program will automatically terminate and report an error.

$$MPSTD \begin{cases} MPSTD \leq 0.03 & \textit{absence of human motion} \\ 0.03 \leq MPSTD \leq 0.2 & \textit{human motion detected} \\ MPSTD \geq 0.4 & \textit{system anomaly detected} \end{cases} \tag{3.6}$$

3.2.3 Doppler Frequency Estimation

Upon detecting human motion, a modified CSIR-based algorithm is employed to estimate the Doppler frequency at this moment. A Mobius transformation-based Doppler frequency estimator is adopted to obtain both the sign and magnitude of Doppler frequency with less complexity [15]. Doppler frequency

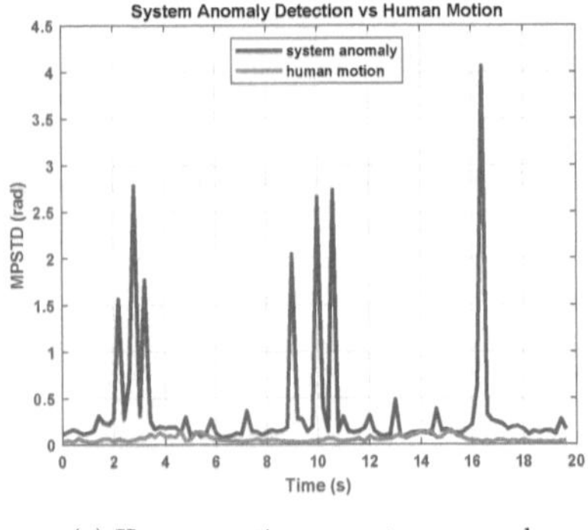 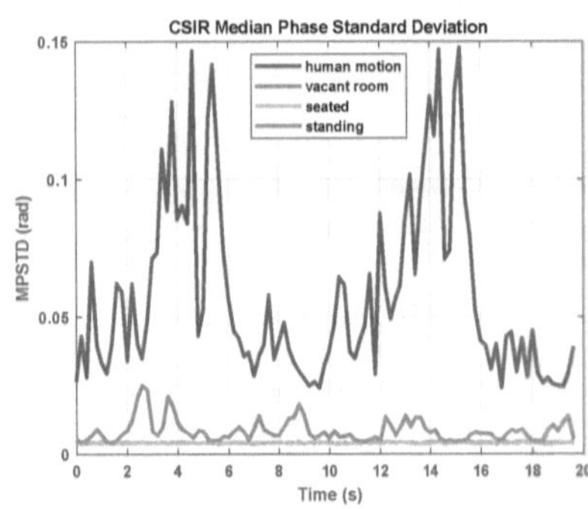

(a) Human motion vs system anomaly   (b) Human motion vs static scenario

Figure 3.3: Median phase standard deviation of CSI ratio samples

in a given sampling window is used further for separating the static and dynamic components in 3.2.4. Moreover, both MPSTD and Doppler frequency estimates in a couple of consecutive sampling windows will be recorded to confirm genuine motion in 3.2.5.

3.2.4   Separation of Static and Dynamic Components

This module is responsible for separating the LoS "dynamic signals" reflected off the human body from the static signals that are not motion-related. Self-correlation of CSI samples is utilized to eliminate random phase shifts induced by clock asynchrony and the resulting separated dynamic components are further utilized for AoA and delay estimation.

3.2.5   Human Motion Confirmation and Exception Handling

Fluctuating signal-to-noise ratio (SNR) of a wireless link makes motion detection susceptible to noise. Hence, this module is designed to confirm genuine human motion and further mitigate risks of false detection. On the one hand, if human motion is detected consistently for a given number of sampling windows, the human localization process is initiated. On the other hand, if the system detects inconsistent motion, it evaluates the median value of the recorded MPSTD to determine whether to wait for more reliable data or restart the program.

3.2.6 AoA and Delay Estimation

This module works to estimate AoA and propagation delay by aggregating data from successive sampling windows, denoted as a "joint window" in this book, after genuine human motion is confirmed. Consequently, the first localization outcome is pending until the number of sampling windows reaches a joint window. The MLE-based estimators [38] are established for parameter estimation, leveraging the separated dynamic components in the preceding module. Once this step is completed, all the motion-related parameters are determined.

3.2.7 Human Target Localization

Given that the location of the UE is known to the BS, the position of a human target is derived geometrically in a planar coordinate system, using AoA and delay estimates. Upon this step, the scheme concludes the localization workflow for a sampling window.

3.3 Parameter Estimation Algorithms

This section presents the details of parameter estimation algorithms for Doppler frequency, AoA, and propagation delay. To tackle the clock asynchrony between transmitters and receivers, this proposed tracking scheme integrates a CSIR-based Doppler frequency estimator with maximum likelihood estimation-based estimators for AoA and delay estimation. To begin with, a signal model is presented first.

3.3.1 Signal Model for Uplink Sensing

In a typical LTE mobile network, a base station (BS) communicates with multiple user equipment (UE). UE here can be fixed broadband access points whose locations are already known to the BS. In the uplink sensing setup, the UE transmits radio frames with uplink pilot signals. The BS receives uplink signals for both communication and sensing. The above general uplink setup is further simplified to a single wireless link with a BS and UE in the demonstration system, illustrated in 3.4. This signal model includes the following three assumptions.

Figure 3.4: Simplified uplink sensing setup

- There is one LoS propagation path for the dynamic signal reflected off the moving target. This LoS signal is much stronger than other non-LoS dynamic signals in strength, so only this LoS path is considered for dynamic signals.
- The static signals that do not reflect on the moving target are orders of magnitude stronger than the LoS dynamic signals in a sampling window.
- The location and AoA of the UE are known to the BS.

In a multi-path channel, signals received by a BS are represented as a superimposition of static signals via L_s propagation paths and one dynamic signal. In a typical MIMO-OFDM system, a baseband signal is modulated by N subcarriers and received by M_R antennas. Assuming that the interval between two consecutive UL pilot symbols is T_A (defined as a snapshot in the sensing scenario), the frequency domain signal received by the m_{th} antenna at the k_{th} snapshot on subcarrier index n_{th} is expressed in (3.7) [15], [35].

$$s\left(f_n, kT_A\right) = H_m^h \exp\left\{j2\pi\left[f_o\left(kT_A\right)kT_A - f_n\tau_o\left(kT_A\right)\right]\right\}$$

$$\times \left\{\sum_{l=1}^{L_s} b_l exp\left(-j2\pi f_n\tau_l\right) \times \mathbf{a}(m, \theta_l) + b_d exp\left[j2\pi\left(f_D kT_A - f_n\tau_d\right)\right] \times \mathbf{a}(m, \theta_d)\right\} \qquad (3.7)$$

$$+ z\left(kT_A, n\right)$$

b_l: complex amplitude of the static signal along the l_{th} propagation path

b_d: complex amplitude of the dynamic signal

k: k_{th} snapshot

T_A: the interval between two consecutive UL pilot symbols

H_m^h: complex amplitude of the m_{th} antenna with its connected transceiver channel

f_n: the n_{th} subcarrier frequency

$f_o\left(kT_A\right)$: carrier frequency offset at kT_A moment

$\tau_o\left(kT_A\right)$: timing offset at kT_A moment.

f_D: Doppler frequency

τ_l, τ_d: propagation delay for static and dynamic paths respectively

$\mathbf{a}(m, \theta_l)$: the steering vector of l_{th} static path for the m_{th} antenna

$\mathbf{a}(m, \theta_d)$: the steering vector of dynamic path for the m_{th} antenna

$z(kT_A)$: additive Gaussian white noise (AGWN) with zero mean and variance of σ^2

3.3.2 Doppler Frequency Estimation

As shown in (3.7), time-variant phase shifts, $exp\{j2\pi[f_o(kT_A)kT_A - f_n\tau_o(kT_A)]\}$ is the same for all the receive antennas at the same symbol. Divide the received signals between two neighbouring antennas, and the CSI ratio (CSIR) of these two antennas is derived in (3.8).

$$
\begin{cases}
R(t) = H^h_{m,m+1} \dfrac{H^s_{n,m}(kT_A) + H^d_{n,m}(kT_A)\,z}{H^s_{n,m+1}(kT_A) + H^d_{n,m+1}(kT_A)\,z} \\[2ex]
z = e^{j2\pi f_D t}
\end{cases}
\tag{3.8}
$$

$H^s_{n,m}(kT_A)$: $\sum_{l=1}^{L_s} b_l exp(-j2\pi f_n\tau_l) \times \mathbf{a}(m,\theta_l)$, dynamic signal component

$H^d_{n,m}(kT_A)$: $b_d exp[j2\pi(f_D kT_A - f_n\tau_d)] \times \mathbf{a}(m,\theta_d)$, static signal component

$H^h_{m,m+1}$: the complex amplitude ratio between m_{th} and $(m+1)_{th}$ receiver channels

As both the static and dynamic signal components are considered approximately unchanged in hundreds of milliseconds, (3.8) maps a unit circle to another of different radius. Since $R(t)$ varies along a circle, a least square method (LSM) is adopted to estimate C_0, which is the coordinate of the circle center on the complex plane. Then, the raw CSIR samples are translated to the origin of the complex plane by subtracting C_0, resulting in new CSI-ratio datasets. Subsequently, weighted linear mapping is applied to find the time variation rate β_1 of the angle of $R(t)$, and Doppler frequency can be expressed as

$$
f_D = \frac{\beta_1}{2\pi T_s}
\tag{3.9}
$$

given the inherent noise in practical signals, the effectiveness of the LSM-based approximation can be compromised in certain scenarios. Therefore, a modified

---

Algorithm 1 Refined Mobius Transform-based Doppler Frequency Estimation

---

Input: A sequence of CSI-ratio samples $R(t_k) = \{R(t_1), R(t_2), ...R(t_N)\}$ within a sampling window

Output: The estimated Doppler frequency f_D for a sampling window

1: Calculate the arithmetic mean, R_0, for the $R(t_k)$ in a sampling window
2: Subtract R_0 from $R(t_k)_{k=1}^{N}$, resulting in $\bar{R}(t_k)_{k=1}^{N}$
3: Calculate the angles of $R(t_k)_{k=1}^{N}$, resulting in a sequence of $\theta_R(t_k)$
4: Estimate the value $\beta_1 = 2\pi T_s f_D$, by using the linear mapping in Section A.1
5: $f_D = \frac{\beta_1}{2pi T_s}$

---

method based on the arithmetic mean of CSI-ratio samples is adopted instead. Specifically, in a sampling window of hundreds of milliseconds, the circle center can be approximated by calculating the arithmetic mean of the raw CSI-ratio samples within that sampling window. The refined algorithm for Doppler frequency is described in Algorithm 1.

3.3.3 CSI Self-correlation and Separation of Static and Dynamic Components

Similar to the cross-antenna-cross-correlation (CACC) method, the self-correlation operation of CSI also eliminates the time-variant phase shifts induced by CFO and TO [38]. CSI self-correlation is defined as the product of CSI data and their conjugates, or channel frequency response (CFR) power. To manifest this, we re-define $s(t)$ here, making it more concise and pertinent to AoA and delay.

$$
\begin{cases}
s(t) = H_m^h \times \ H_n^e(t) \times \left[H_{n,m}^s(t) + H_{n,m}^{d'}(t) \right] \\[2mm]
H_n^e(t) = exp\left\{ j2\pi \left[f_o(t)t - f_n\tau_o(t) \right] \right\} \\[2mm]
H_{n,m}^s(t) = \displaystyle\sum_{l=1}^{L_s} b_l exp\left(-j2\pi f_n \tau_l \right) \times \mathbf{a}\left(\mathbf{m}, \theta_1 \right) \\[4mm]
H_{n,m}^{d'}(t) = b_d exp\left\{ -j2\pi \dfrac{f_n}{c} \left[d^d + c\dfrac{f_D}{f_c}(k-1)T_A + d_{m,1} sin\theta^d \right] \right\}
\end{cases}
\tag{3.10}
$$

where $d^d = c\tau^d$ is the propagation distance and $d_{m,1}$ refers to the spacing between the m_{th} antenna element and the 1_{st} antenna element. In particular, the dynamic component, $H_{n,m}^{d'}(t)$, is formulated so that it encompasses Doppler frequency, propagation distance, and AoA of the dynamic LoS signal. Since a sampling window typically lasts hundreds of milliseconds, we assume that a person moves at a constant speed within a sampling window. Consequently, the distance at k_{th} snapshot is approximately $d^d(k) = d^d + c\frac{f_D}{f_n}(k-1)\Delta t$, while the AoA is considered unchanged. These relationships lay a foundation for AoA and distance estimation for each sampling window. Based on (3.10), the CSI self-correlation is derived in (3.11), where the power of H_n^e equals 1. Hereafter, the notation (t) is dropped for brevity.

$$
\begin{aligned}
\|s(t)\|^2 &= \left(H_n^e H_m^h \right)\left(H_{n,m}^s + H_{n,m}^{d'} \right)\left(\overline{H}_n^e \overline{H}_m^h \right)\left(\overline{H}_{n,m}^s + \overline{H}_{n,m}^{d'} \right) \\[2mm]
&= \underbrace{\left\| H_n^e H_m^h H_{n,m}^s \right\|^2}_{staic\ component\ power} + \underbrace{\left\| H_n^e H_m^h \right\|^2 \left[2\left\| H_{n,m}^s H_{n,m}^{d'} \right\| \cos\angle\left(\overline{H}_{n,m}^s H_{n,m}^{d'} \right) + \left\| H_{n,m}^{d'} \right\|^2 \right]}_{dynamic\ component\ power}
\end{aligned}
\tag{3.11}
$$

As shown in (3.11), the time-variant phase shifts are removed. Moreover, it is clearly demonstrated that the CFR power is constituted by a static component and a dynamic component. The dynamic component will be further processed for the estimation of AoA and delay of the LoS dynamic signal. Based on the first assumption that the LoS dynamic component is much stronger than its NLoS counterpart, the term $\left\| H_{n,m}^{d'} \right\|^2$ is omitted hereafter. Thus, the refined formulation is written below.

$$\begin{cases} \left\| H_n^e H_m^h H_{n,m}^s \right\|^2 = u_{n,m} \\[2mm] 2\left\| H_n^e H_m^h \right\|^2 \left\| H_{n,m}^s H_{n,m}^{d'} \right\| \cos \angle \left(\overline{H}_{n,m}^s H_{n,m}^{d'} \right) \approx v_{n,m,k} \end{cases} \tag{3.12}$$

In [44], a highpass filter is used to extract the dynamic component induced by respiration since the static signals remain unchanged in a sampling window. However, it is challenging to determine an appropriate cutoff frequency that does not significantly affect the relatively weaker dynamic signals. Instead, WiDFS [38] introduces a method similar to the coherent accumulation technique used in radar signal processing. This method treats the static component in a way analogous to coherent echo signals in consecutive snapshots. Specifically, the static component, $u_{(n,m)}$, is approximated by the arithmetic mean of CFR power in a sampling window. Consequently, the dynamic component, $v_{n,m,k}$, is retrieved by subtracting $u_{n,m}$ from the total CFR for each CSI sample. This is represented in (3.13), where K_{win} refers to the length of a sampling window. The subcript k is the index number of the snapshots in a sampling window.

$$\begin{cases} u_{n,m} = \dfrac{1}{N_p} \sum_{k=1}^{K_{win}} \left\| CSI_{n,m.k} \right\|^2 \\[4mm] v_{n,m.k} = \left\| CSI_{n,m.k} \right\|^2 - u_{n,m} \end{cases} \tag{3.13}$$

3.3.4 AoA and Propagation Delay Estimation

In this scheme, AoA and propagation delay of dynamic signals are estimated only when persistent human movement is detected to avoid erroneous estimates. To acquire AoA and delay estimates individually, the MLE-based method is adopted by utilizing the static and dynamic components in (3.13). The detailed derivations are presented in Section A.2, and only some of the key results are listed in this section. Divide $v_{n,m,k}$ by $u_{(}n,m)$, and the quotient results in (3.14).

$$\begin{cases} \dfrac{v_{n,m,k}}{u_{n,m}} = x_{n,m}\cos\left[2\pi f^D (k-1) T_A\right] + y_{n,m}\sin\left[2\pi f^D (k-1) T_A\right] \\[2ex] x_{n,m} = 2\left\|\dfrac{H_{n,m,k}^{d'}}{H_{n,m}^s}\right\|\cos\left\{\angle\overline{H}_{n,m}^s - 2\pi\dfrac{f_n}{c}\left[d^d + d_{m,1}\sin\theta^d\right]\right\} \\[2ex] y_{n,m} = 2\left\|\dfrac{H_{n,m,k}^{d'}}{H_{n,m}^S}\right\|\sin\left\{\angle\overline{H}_{n,m}^s - 2\pi\dfrac{f_n}{c}\left[d^d + d_{m,1}\sin\theta^d\right]\right\} \end{cases} \tag{3.14}$$

Since f_D is already estimated, an equation set can be formulated for different snapshots in a sampling window, and it is solved via a least square method. Consequently, a pair of $(x_{n,m}, y_{n,m})$ results from the solution. In order to formulate an MLE function pertinent to AoA and delay, we define $Z_{n,m,k}^{s,d}$ as a weighted phase shift based on the quotient of $\frac{y_{n,m}}{x_{n,m}}$. The weight is relevant to $r_{n,m,k}$, the residual of the solution to (A.8). This is derived in (3.15).

$$\begin{cases} Z_{n,m,k}^{s,d} = w_{n,m,k}e^{j\arctan2(y_{n,m},x_{n,m})} = w_{n,m,k}e^{j\left\{\angle\overline{H_{n,m}^s}-2\pi\frac{f_n}{c}\left[d^d+d_{m,1}\sin\theta^d\right]\right\}} \\[2ex] \angle\overline{H_{n,m}^s} = 2\pi\dfrac{f_n}{c}\left(d_1^s + d_{m,1}\times sin\theta^s\right) \\[2ex] w_{n,m,k} = \left\{\dfrac{2}{\pi}\times\left[\dfrac{\pi}{2} - \arctan\left(\dfrac{r_{n,m,k}}{K_{win}}\right)\right]\right\}^3 \end{cases} \tag{3.15}$$

where $\angle H_{n,m}^s$ is the phase delay of a static LoS path between the transmit antenna and the m_{th} receive antenna. According to A.3, the term $\angle H_{n,m}^s$ can also be expressed in (3.16).

$$\angle H_{n,m}^s = -2\pi\dfrac{f_n}{c}d_1^s + \Delta\varphi_{1,m}^h - \angle U_{1,m} \tag{3.16}$$

where $\angle U_{1,m}$ is the angle of the static components of the CSI cross-correlation between the 1_{st} antenna and the m_{th} antenna. Since the UE's location is already known to the BS, $\angle H_{n,m}^s$ is a known constant. Multiplying $Z_{n,m,k}^{s,d}$ by $e^{J\angle H_{n,m}^s}$ results in $Z_{n,m,k}^d$ in (3.17). As is shown, the static component is completely removed and $Z_{n,m,k}^d$ is merely associated with AoA and delay of the dynamic signals. Therefore, we name it 'Refined Dynamic Component Phase'.

$$Z_{n,m,k}^d = Z_{n,m,k}^{s,d} e^{J\angle H_{n,m}^s} = w_{n,m,k} e^{-j2\pi \frac{f_n}{c}\left[d^d + d_{m,1}\sin\theta^d\right]} \tag{3.17}$$

As practical wireless links are impacted by noise that threatens the localization accuracy, $Z_{n,m,k}^d$ from adjacent sampling windows are aggregated to achieve reliable estimates of AoA and delay in this proposed scheme. Figure 3.5 illustrates the way the data from these joint windows are aggregated. Via these joint windows, MLE methods are applied respectively for AoA and delay estimations in (3.18) and (3.19).

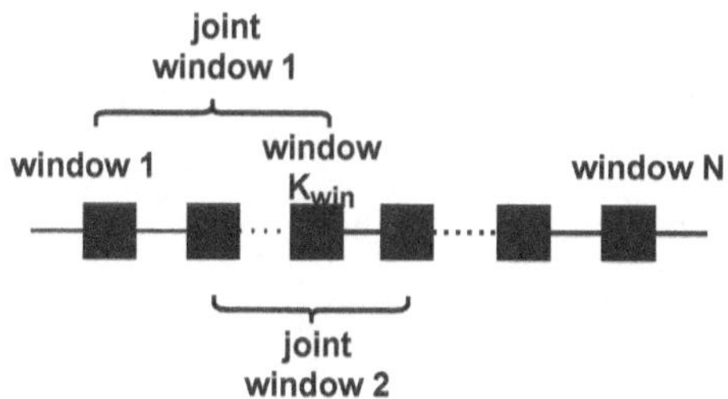

Figure 3.5: Joint windows

$$\underset{\theta^d \in [\theta^{min}, \theta^{max}]}{\arg\max} \sum_{k=1}^{K} \sum_{n=1}^{N} \left\| \sum_{m=1}^{M} Z_{n,m,k}^d e^{j2\pi \frac{f_n}{c} d_{m,1}\sin\theta^d} \right\| \tag{3.18}$$

(3.18) aims to discover θ^d, the AoA within a range of angles that maximizes the above function.

$$\begin{cases} \underset{d^d \in \left(d_{min}^X, d_{max}^X\right]}{\arg\max} \sum_{k=1}^{K} \sum_{m=1}^{M} \left\| \sum_{n=1}^{N} Z_{n,m,k}^d Z^D e^{j2\pi \frac{f_n}{c} d^d} \right\| \\ Z^D = e^{J2\pi \sum_{1}^{K} \frac{f_D \times c}{f_c}(l-1)\Delta t} \end{cases} \tag{3.19}$$

Likewise, (3.19) aims to search d^d, the most probable delay within the range of interest. Since a person moves a distance in each sampling window, this displacement is compensated for by $\sum_l^K \frac{f_D}{f_c} \times c(l-1)\Delta t$. Thus, the term Z^D accounts for phase delay due to human motion.

Algorithm 2 AoA and delay Estimation based on weighted residual quotient

---

Input:

- Doppler frequency sequence in the latest joint window $\{f_D(W_k)\} = \{f_D(W_1), f_D(W_2)...f_D(W_{N_r})\}$
- CSI samples in the latest joint window $\{CSI(W_k)\}$
- AoA search range and increment: $[\theta_{min}, \theta_{max}], \Delta\theta^d$
- delay search range and increment: $[d^d_{min}, d^d_{max}], \Delta d^d$

Output: AoA and probation delay for the latest sampling

1: **if** Human motion is detected **then**

2:     Solve the equation in (A.8) and obtain $x_{n,m,k}$, $y_{n,m,k}$, $r_{n,m,k}$

3:     Calculate $Z^d_{n,m,k}$ using (3.17)

4:     Follow motion confirmation procedure in Sec. 3.2.5

5: **else if** Human motion is undetected **then**

6:     Follow motion confirmation procedure in Sec. 3.2.5

7: **end if**

8: **if** Human motion is confirmed **then**

9:     Estimate AoA of LoS dynamic signals using (3.18)

10:     Estimate delay of LoS dynamic signals using (3.19)

11: **else if** Absence of human motion is confirmed **then**

12:     Display 'Absence of human motion' and restart the program

13: **end if**

In summary, the algorithm for AoA and delay estimation is presented in Algorithm 2.

3.3.5 Human Target Localization

In a typical sensing scenario illustrated in Figure 3.6, the human target, the
transmitter, and the receiver form a triangle. In this planar representation, θ^s
and $Dist\_TR$ are pre-defined constants and d^d, θ^d are estimated. Locate 0_{th}
antenna at the origin, the distance between a target and the origin is calculated
via the Cosine Rule. A moving target is then positioned by solving (3.20).

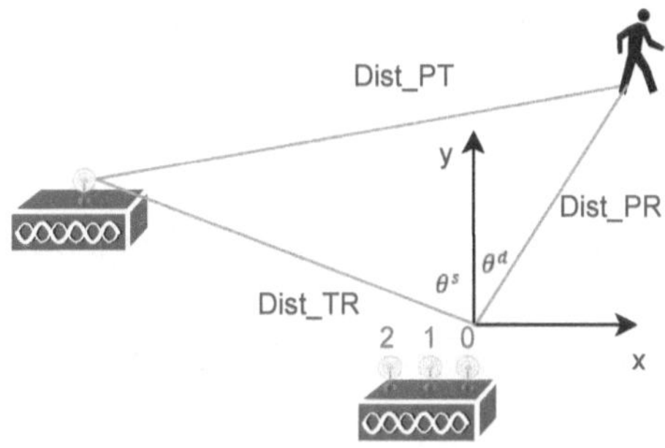

Figure 3.6: Human target localization

$$
\begin{cases}
Dist\_PR = \dfrac{\left(d^d\right)^2 - (Dist\_TR)^2}{2\left[d^d - Dist\_TR \times \cos\left(\theta^d - \theta^s\right)\right]} \\[2ex]
Pos\_X = Dist\_PR \times \sin\theta^d \\[2ex]
Pos\_Y = Dist\_PR \times \cos\theta^d
\end{cases}
\tag{3.20}
$$

3.4 Parameter Study Selection of K_{win} and K_{JW}

Both the sampling window size, K_{win}, and the joint window size, K_{JW} are
critical parameters for localization performance. Hence, this section presents
a parametric study of these two parameters. This section examines the impacts of both parameters on Doppler frequency, AoA, tracking accuracy and
computation time.

3.4.1 Impact of Sampling Window Size

Based on the algorithms introduced in 3.3, the sampling window size, K_{win}, directly impacts Doppler frequency estimates. Combined with joint window size, K_{JW}, it also affects AoA and delay estimation. On the one hand, the CSIR-based Doppler frequency estimator prefers a larger K_{win} for more accurate estimates. On the other hand, the computation time rises with the increase of K_{win}, consequently compromising the real-time performance. Therefore, there is a trade-off between tracking accuracy and real-time performance when selecting an appropriate value of K_{win}. Besides, a prolonged sampling window leads to large latency in positioning and also affects localization accuracy.

The impacts of K_{win} on the estimation of Doppler frequency, AoA and computation time are illustrated in Figure 3.7. The CSI samples used in this study are collected in a tracking test along a V-line trajectory. The data are processed offline.

Table 3.1: Impact of K_{win} and K_{JW} on the running time

K_{win}	K_{JW}	95% running time (millisecond)
100	10	49.0
200	10	68.8
300	10	79.1
400	10	108.6
200	5	56.0
200	15	80.7

The impact on Doppler frequency estimation aligns with the theoretical predictions that a larger sampling window results in more accurate estimates. As is shown in Figure 3.7(a), where a window size of 100 leads to pronounced fluctu-

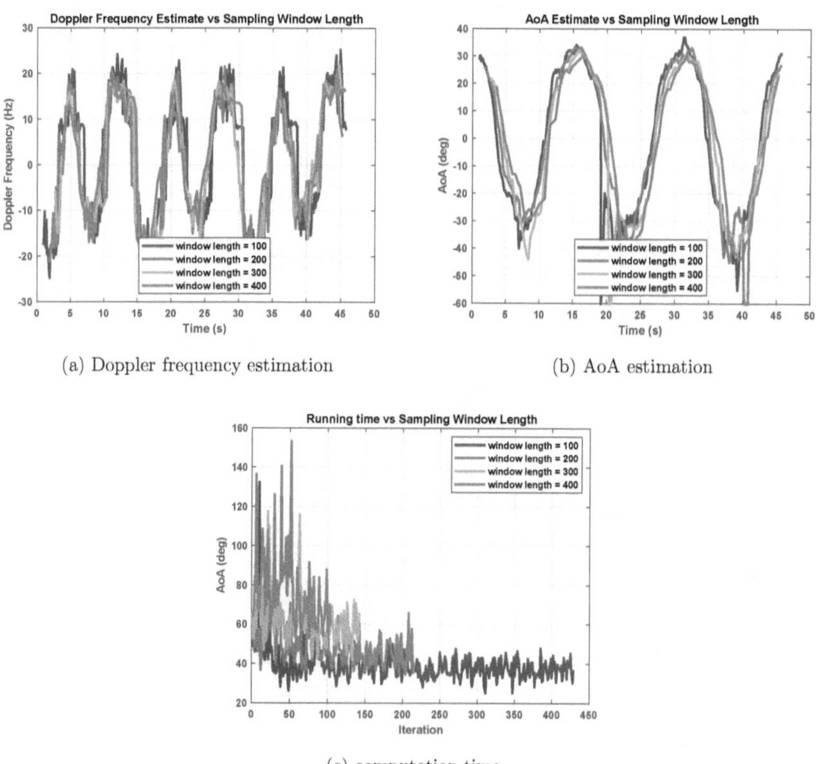

(a) Doppler frequency estimation   (b) AoA estimation

(c) computation time

Figure 3.7: Impact of K_{win} on Doppler frequency, AoA and computation time, $(K_{JW} = 10)$

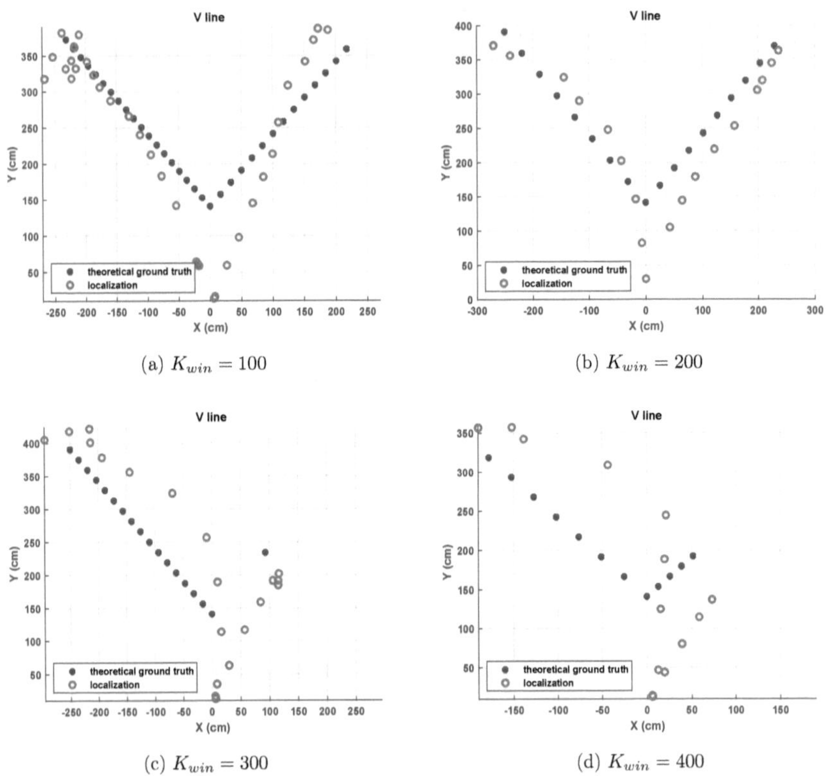

(a) $K_{win} = 100$

(b) $K_{win} = 200$

(c) $K_{win} = 300$

(d) $K_{win} = 400$

Figure 3.8: Impact of K_{win} on localization accuracy: $K_{JW} = 10$
V-line trajectory

ations and abrupt shifts in the Doppler frequency curve, potentially leading to erroneous delay estimates. In comparison, the curve becomes much smoother as K_{win} exceeds 200. On the other hand, AoA estimation seems less insensitive to the value of K_{win} than Doppler frequency, as demonstrated by Figure 3.7(b). It is worth noting that K_{win} also has a significant impact on the running time of the program. Table 3.2 lists the 95% running time versus K_{win}. The results indicate that a larger sampling window inevitably jeopardizes real-time performance. However, there is a limitation on the running time for real-time implementation, depending on the data sampling rate and displaying latency. As a design trade-off, a shorter sampling window is preferred on the condition that it satisfies the requirement of localization accuracy.

Table 3.2: Impact of K_{win} and K_{JW} on the localization errors

window length (msec)	joint window	x axis (cm)		y axis (cm)	
		50%	80%	50%	80%
100	10	27	81	55	83
200	10	21	44	18	52
300	10	83	104	47	126
400	10	19	66	64	118
200	5	26	37	19	49
200	15	8	30	26	49

The influence of K_{win} on the localization accuracy is shown in Figure 3.8. Table 3.2 provides the 50% and 80% localization errors on both axes. According to Figure 3.8 and the corresponding data in Table 3.2, the sampling window size of 200 milliseconds results in the best localization performance, while the localization errors increase with the sampling window size of 300 and 400 milliseconds. The reason can be analyzed as the following. A prolonged window size results in higher latency in which a person moves a longer distance, thus resulting in increased deviations from his true position. As a trade-off, the sampling window size is optimized as 200 milliseconds.

3.4.2 Impact of Joint Window Size

The joint window size, K_{JW}, exerts an impact on the estimation of AoA and delay. Besides, it determines the latency for the first localization estimate. Figure 3.9 presents the AoA estimation and running time versus K_{JW}. As is shown, Fluctuations appear evident in the AoA curve with the joint window size of 5, which is insufficient to provide an accurate estimate. By contrast, a larger window size above such as 10 or 15 ensures more stable and reliable estimates. As is presented in Table 3.1, the running time slightly rises with an increased K_{JW}. Figure 3.10 illustrates the localized trajectories versus K_{JW} when the window size is 200 milliseconds. As expected by the algorithm, a larger joint window size seems to monotonically result in stable estimates. However, experimental results show that when K_{JW} surpasses 8, the improvement in localization precision is insignificant. On the other hand, a larger joint window size induces a longer computation time.

Based on a comprehensive evaluation of the impacts of K_{win} and K_{JW} on the tracking accuracy and computation time, an optimized combination of these two parameters is selected as $K_{win} = 200$ and $K_{JW} = 8$.

3.5 Conclusion

This chapter introduces a robust and efficient human motion detection and tracking scheme for the demonstrator. The proposed scheme is characterized

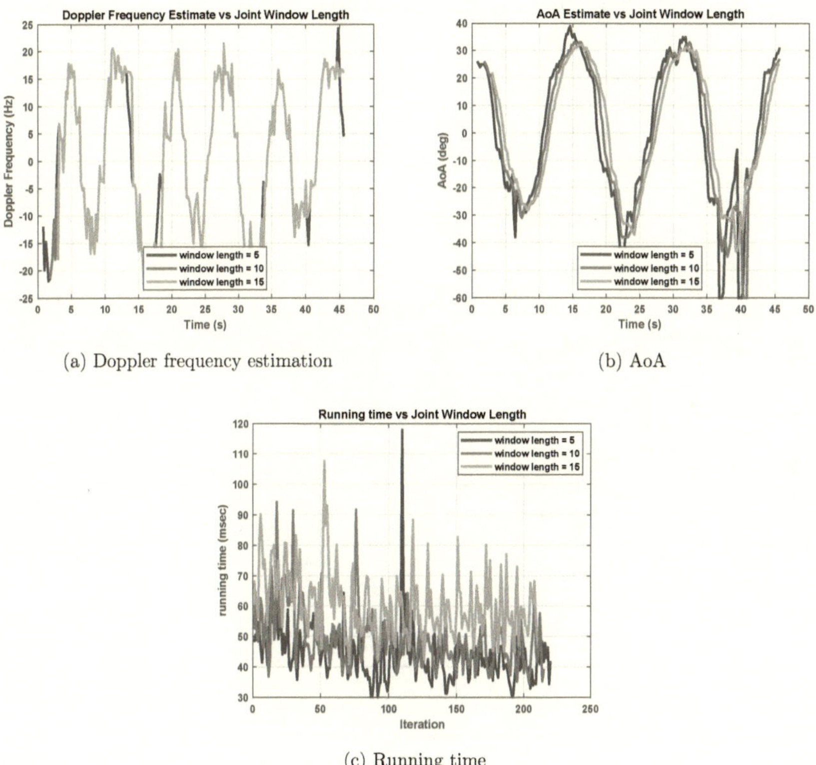

(a) Doppler frequency estimation

(b) AoA

(c) Running time

Figure 3.9: Impact of K_{JW} on Doppler frequency,AoA and running time,$K_{win} = 200$

by a well-structured workflow and lightweight parameter estimation algorithms for Doppler frequency, AoA and propagation delay. By evaluating the impact of K_{win} and K_{JW} on the localization accuracy and computation time, an optimized parameter combination is determined for the implementation of this proposed scheme. The offline tests manifest that the proposed scheme enables tracking in real-time with 95% of running time less than 70 milliseconds.

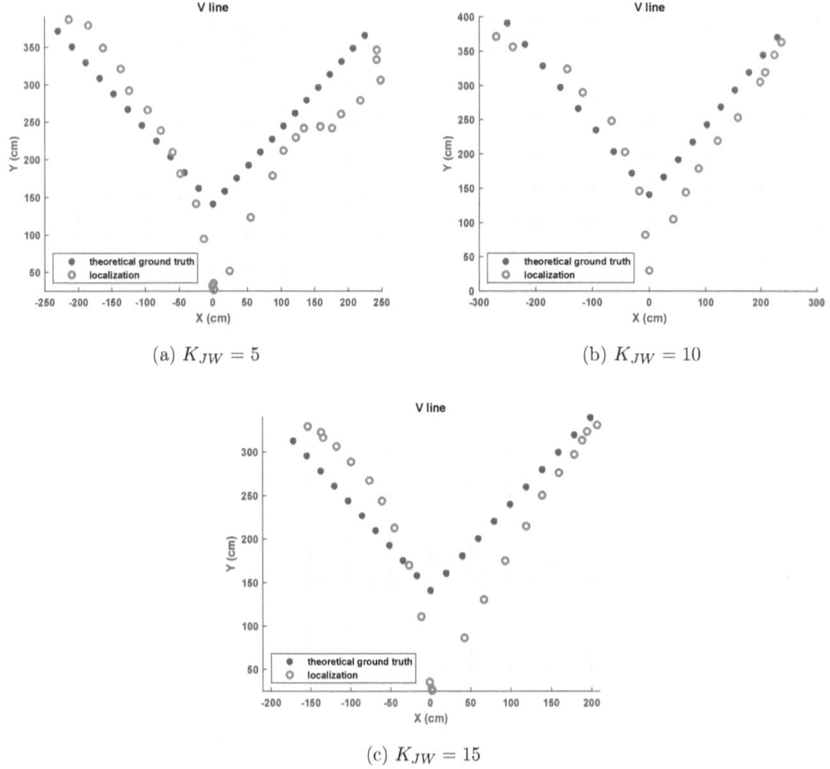

(a) $K_{JW} = 5$

(b) $K_{JW} = 10$

(c) $K_{JW} = 15$

Figure 3.10: Impact of K_{JW} on localization accuracy: $K_{win} = 200$
V-line trajectory

Chapter 4

Design and Implementation of the Demonstration System

4.1 Introduction

This chapter details the implementation of this real-time human motion detection and tracking demonstrator. This demonstrator is implemented on the National Instrument (NI) Massive MIMO prototyping test bed. The implementation primarily focuses on two aspects. The first part is dedicated to developing a customized pilot-streaming interface which prepares and streams active pilot samples to a target-tracking module running on the same controller machine. The second part focuses on the implementation of the target-tracking module. Section 4.2 presents an overview of this demonstrator, including the system setup and its operational procedures. Section 4.3 introduces the signal structure employed in this demonstrator. Section 4.4 elaborates on the development of the pilot-streaming interface. Section 4.5 covers the software development of the target-tracking module. Section 4.6 summarizes the work in this chapter.

4.2   System Overview

4.2.1   System Setup and Operational Procedures

Figure 4.1 illustrates the high-level block diagram of this demonstration system. It mainly comprises the Massive MIMO prototyping test bed as the BS and a USRP device as the UE. The supporting MIMO Framework Application (MFA) software packages running on both the BS and UE controllers are responsible for the configuration of an LTE-based communication link. Through the configuration of the MFA, an LTE link is set up with a customized LTE-based signal structure. In this passive localization system, the BS has a linear array of three receive antennas, each connected to its corresponding transceiver. The UE has a single transmit antenna. The software implementation of the demonstrator involves a pilot-streaming interface and a target-tracking module, both operating on the BS controller. Once an LTE link is set up, the received LTE pilot samples are streamed on demand to the target-tracking module via the pilot-streaming interface. Simultaneously, the target-tracking module reads the received pilots and undertakes target tracking. Once tracking is completed for a sampling window, the updated localization result will be instantly displayed on the monitor.

4.2.2   Hardware Development Platform and Software Implementation Environment

To seamlessly integrate this demonstrator with the framework of an LTE communication link, the National Instrument (NI) Massive MIMO prototyping system is leveraged as the development platform [45]. The BS test bed encompasses 16 transceivers in total, a test bed controller, and timing and clock synchronization modules. A timing and synchronization module (PXIe-6674T) and a timing and clock distribution module (CDA-2990) enable all the BS transceivers to be synchronized in clock and carrier frequency. In addition, the UE comprises 2 transceivers in total and a desktop computer as a controller. The hardware setup diagrams for the BS and UE are illustrated in Figure 4.2.

The MAF software package implements an orthogonal frequency division multiplexing (OFDM) physical layer with LTE time-division duplex (TDD) specifications. The MAF enables a configurable LTE radio frame structure, and modifiable modulation schemes ranging from QPSK to 256-QAM. By configuring the software, we can also specify the center frequency, receiver gain and transmitter power supported by the USRP hardware. The spatial layers for transmission can also be activated on demand. In addition, implemented in LabVIEW Communications System Design Suite, the MAF provides an open,

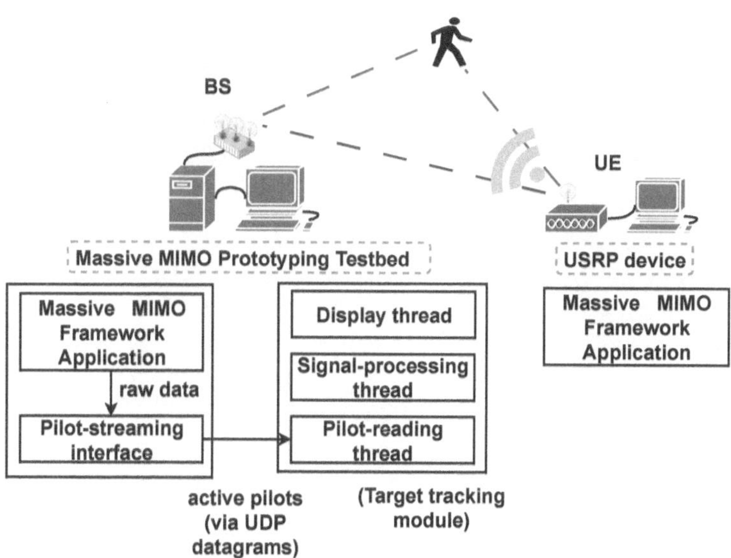

Figure 4.1: High-level diagram of the demonstration system

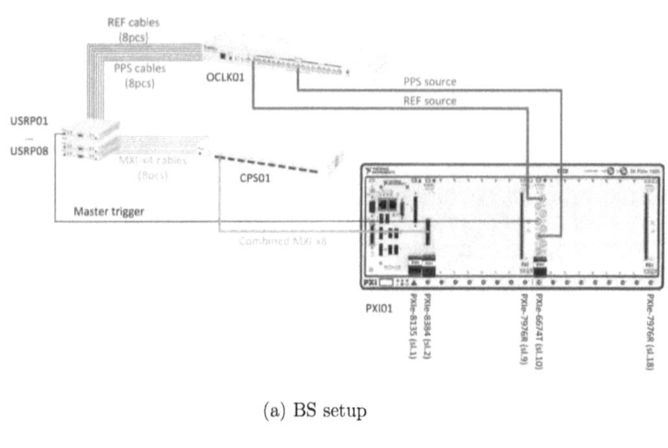

(a) BS setup

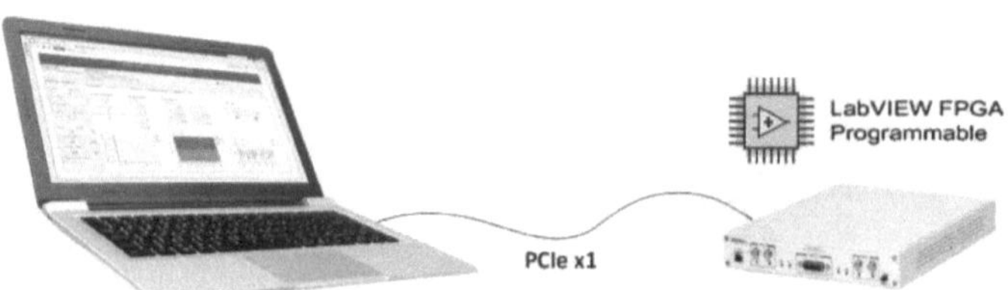

(b) UE setup

Figure 4.2: Hardware setup for the BS and UE [45]

modular, and modifiable software development environment so that additional functional modules can be implemented in the MAF. Figure4.3 shows the software control panels for the BS and UE respectively.

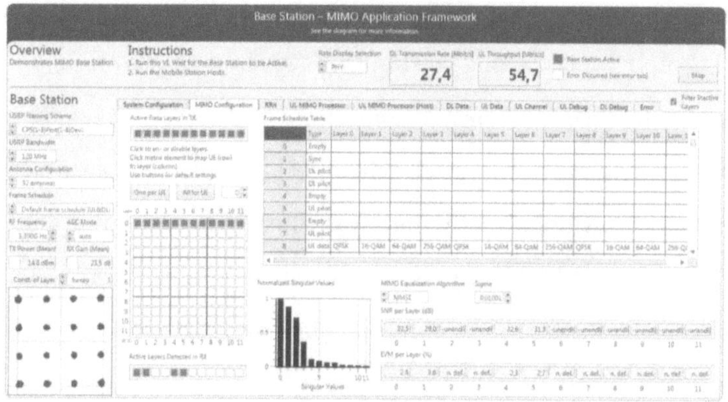

(a) BS control panel

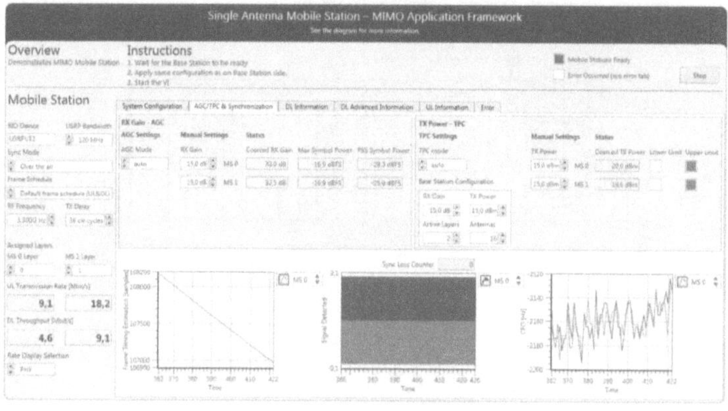

(b) UE control panel

Figure 4.3: MIMO Framework Application interface for BS and UE [45]

4.3 Signal Structure

4.3.1 Uplink Pilot Signal Structure

The uplink pilot signal, proposed as a waveform candidate for radio sensing
[5], is leveraged for CSI-based localization in this demonstration system. The
uplink pilot sequence is designed for uplink channel state estimation and equal-
ization. The uplink pilot signal used in this system is derived from a length-300
QPSK sequence, which is repeated four times and results in a length-1200 sequence, corresponding to the used 1200 subcarriers in a typical LTE system.
The spectrum of an uplink LTE signal is illustrated in Figure 4.4 [14]. The
channel bandwidth is 20 MHz and the subcarrier spacing is 15 KHz. The uplink subcarrier frequency, f_{sub}^{UL}, is represented by (4.2). Here, f_c refers to the
center frequency and N_{ind}^{UL} refers to the uplink subcarrier frequency index.

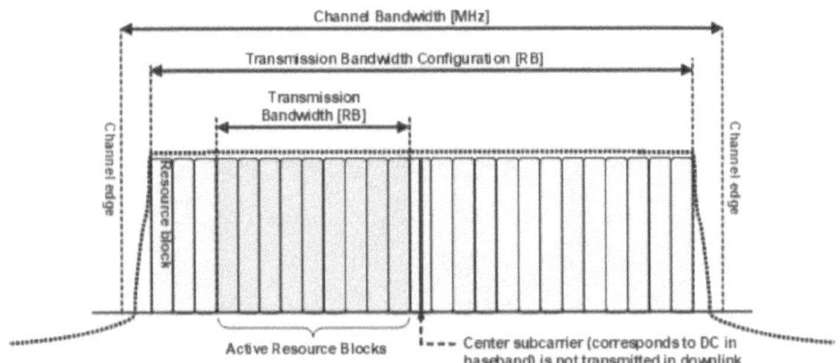

Figure 4.4: LTE signal spectrum [14]

$$f_{sub}^{UL} = f_c \pm 7.5 \times N_{ind}^{UL}, \quad N_{ind}^{UL} : 1, 2, ...600 \tag{4.1}$$

The pilot sequences are mapped to 12 different spatial layers in an OFDM
scheme, as depicted in Figure 4.5. Consequently, pilots corresponding to 12

spatial layers are alternatively mapped to 12 neighbouring subcarriers in a resource block. Since only one spatial layer is activated for transmission at the UE in this demonstrator, 100 out of 1200 subcarriers are modulated with effective pilots while others are padded with nulls. Hence, the subcarrier spacing is 180 KHz. Nevertheless, all of the 1200 subcarriers are transmitted, resulting in voluminous data received at the BS.

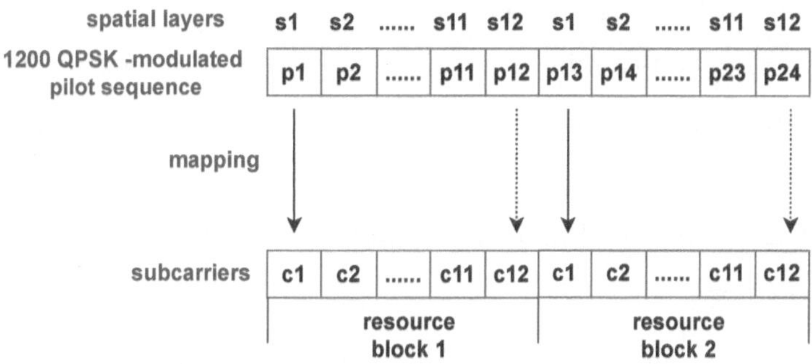

Figure 4.5: Mapping of pilot sequence to subcarriers

4.3.2 Radio Frame Format

The MAF employs a standard 3GPP LTE radio frame in TDD mode as shown in Figure 4.6. A radio frame endures 10 ms and comprises 10 subframes, while each subframe comprises two slots of 0.5 ms in duration. A slot is further broken down into 7 OFDM symbols. Specifically, this demonstration system is configured to contain a single uplink pilot symbol in each slot. As a result, the interval between two pilot signals is 0.5 ms, which corresponds to the data sampling rate of 2 KHz.

4.4   Design and Implementation of the Pilot-streaming Interface

An efficient and effective pilot-streaming interface and a pilot-reading module
are the prerequisites for this CSI-based tracking demonstrator to achieve real-
time performance. Unlike the availability of mature CSI-reading tools in Wi-
Fi-based applications, there are no existing CSI-extracting tools for the NI
Massive MIMO prototyping test bed employed in this demonstrator. Therefore,
a concurrent pilot-streaming interface integrated with a pilot-reading module
has to be developed to this specified end.

4.4.1   Challenges in the Implementation of the Pilot-streaming Interface

The MAF streams all of the received pilots from 16 BS antennas to the BS
controller at the data sampling rate of 2 KHz. This refers to 200 pilot symbols
to be streamed to the controller's memory once per 100 ms. Since each I/Q
symbol is represented by a U32 word (16 bits for each I and Q signal), the data

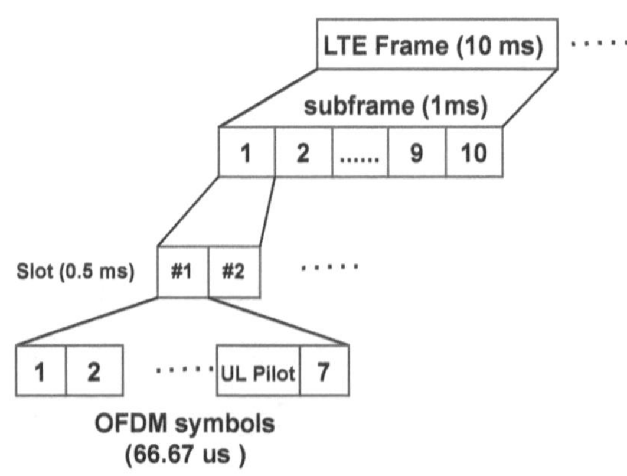

Figure 4.6: Frame structure employed in the demonstrator

size amounts to 15,360,000 Bytes per 100 ms. It is these massive data that make the implementation of a pilot-streaming interface challenging. The major problems and proposed solutions are clarified below.

The first challenge arises due to the massive number of "inactive" pilots. On the one hand, although only one spatial layer is activated for transmission and 3 out of 16 antennas are utilized for this demonstrator, all of the 1200 pilots throughout 12 spatial layers are received in the multiplexed scheme from 16 antenna ports. Consequently, a significant proportion of the received pilots are zero-padded. Even though LabView Communications Suite offers a customized User Datagram Protocol (UDP) block for external data exchange, it is highly beyond the UDP block's capability to promptly accommodate such intensive data transmission. The transmission capability of UDP is constrained by the maximum transmission unit (MTU), allowing only 1500 Bytes per datagram. Alternatively, resorting to partitioning the datasets into numerous short datagrams will induce unacceptable latency in data transfer, preventing the demonstrator from running in real time. On the other hand, the complex arrangement of original pilots hinders efficient CSI-based signal processing. Hence, it is essential to incorporate a pre-processing module to select and re-order the "active" pilots to streamline pilot streaming and signal processing.

The second challenge results from a mismatch between the original data sampling rate and the computation overheads of the tracking scheme. The transceivers stream 200 pilot symbols, namely 200 CSI samples, to the controller's memory once every 100 ms. However, Section 3.4 shows that the computation overhead ranges from 50 ms to 70 ms for processing these 200 CSI samples. Additionally, extra time overheads must be considered for sending the active pilots to the UDP port and displaying. Consequently, the tracking module encounters a very stringent temporal constraint to concurrently perform tracking and read raw CSI samples within a 100-millisecond framework. This disparity in data rate will lead to unpredictable data loss and threaten the reliability of tracking results. To address this challenge, the data are down-sampled to 1 KHz by discarding every other pilot symbol sample. Meanwhile, a buffer queue mechanism is devised to facilitate the down-sampling process and avoid data loss. This measure has been proven to effectively mitigate the timing disparities.

4.4.2 Workflow of the Pilot-streaming Interface

The pilot-streaming interface is designed to meet the following requirements:

- Streaming the pilot data on demand with a configurable duration
- Down-sampling the data rate to 1 KHz
- Ensuring no data loss in transmission

To streamline the workflow and facilitate the experimental evaluations, this pilot-streaming interface is modelled and implemented via a finite state machine (FSM) that comprises 4 states, represented by "Idle", "UDP open", "Wait", "UDP write", and "UDP close". The transition among the states is illustrated in Fig 4.7, delivering an overview of the workflow of this FSM model.

The "Idle" state refers to the state in which streaming is in progress. Each time the system finishes streaming, it returns to this state. When streaming is initiated by a user, the machine shifts to the "UDP open" state where it initializes a specified UDP port. Following initialization, the system automatically transitions to the "Wait" state. This state is designed to facilitate the experiments. In the "Wait" state, the test bed waits for a user-defined period

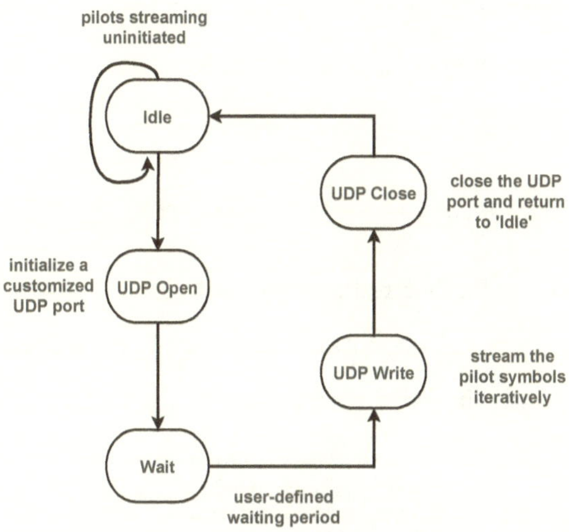

Figure 4.7: Finite State Machine model for the pilot-streaming interface

until the user is prepared for the experiments. When the specified time elapses, a signal is sent to a pilot-reading module within the MAF to start pilot streaming. The system simultaneously shifts to the "UDP write" state. At this stage, the module selects and re-orders active pilots from voluminous pilot samples, and then streams the re-ordered active pilot samples to the UDP port. Streaming is on-demand with a configurable duration. Once streaming finishes, the machine enters the "UDP close" state where the interface dispatches a signal via the UDP datagrams to prompt the tracking module to stop running. Subsequently, the "UDP close" state terminates the UDP streaming and reverts to the 'Idle' state. The entire process operates in a closed-loop fashion and works on demand.

4.4.3 Active Pilots Selecting and Re-ordering

The data size of raw pilot symbols is 153,600 Bytes per millisecond, and these data encompass a complete set of 1200 subcarriers from 16 antenna ports. Nevertheless, if only one spatial layer is activated and 3 receive antennas are utilized in this demonstrator, the data size of the active pilots can be significantly reduced as shown in (4.2)

$$\frac{1}{12} \times \frac{3}{16} \times 153,600 = 2400 \quad \textit{Bytes per ms} \tag{4.2}$$

This data size can be further reduced by half to 1200 Bytes per ms if downsampling is implemented. This notable shrinkage in data size makes it realistic for uninterrupted and efficient data transmission via UDP datagrams.

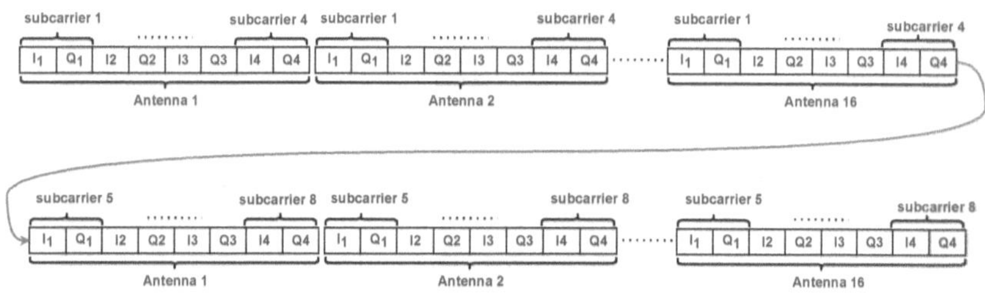

Figure 4.8: Original subcarriers data format

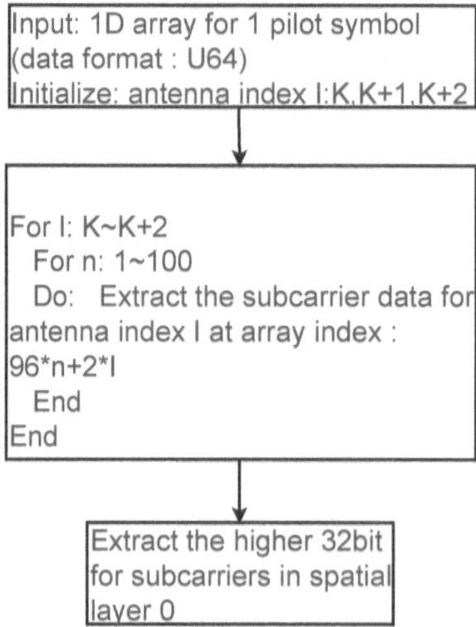

Figure 4.9: Active pilots selecting and re-ordering module

Furthermore, the subcarriers from different antennas are organized in an interleaved arrangement as illustrated in Figure 4.8. Each set of four successive subcarriers, associated with a specific antenna is grouped, whereas subcarrier groups that are attributed to different antennas are sequentially interleaved. An active pilot selecting and re-ordering module (APSR module) is therefore designed to streamline signal processing and reduce computation overheads. Its workflow is presented in Figure 4.9. Consequently, all subcarriers corresponding to the same antenna are re-organized to form a continuous sequence.

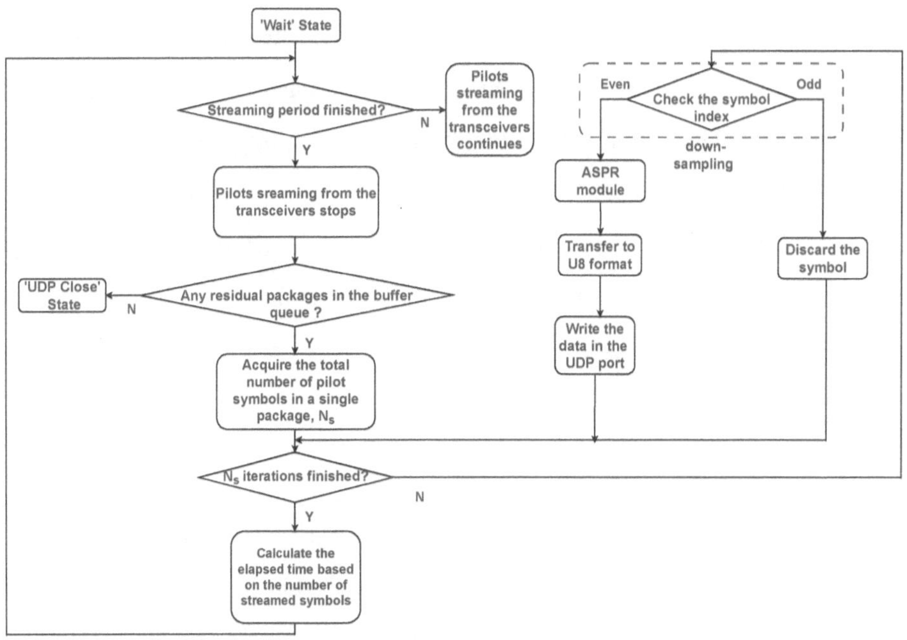

Figure 4.10: 'UDP' Write state

4.4.4 Pilot-streaming via UDP Transmission

This section presents the procedure and techniques applied to real-time pilot streaming via UDP transmission, implemented in the "UDP write" state.

The flowchart outlining the pilot streaming procedure is depicted in Figure 4.10. The pilot samples are streamed from the transceivers in packages, each containing 200 pilots, into a local queue at a data sampling rate of 2 KHz. Once receiving the pilot packages, the "UDP write" module parses each package to individual pilot symbols and processes a single symbol per iteration. This procedure is followed by a down-sampling process to reduce the data sampling rate by half. Subsequently, the down-sampled pilots are transmitted to the APSR module responsible for filtering out the inactive pilot symbols. Eventually, the active pilot symbols are retained and forwarded to a customized UDP port. To implement the streaming control, a timing mechanism is devised, correlating the elapsed time with the number of symbols streamed from the transceivers. When the specific streaming period is reached, streaming from the transceivers is terminated at once whereas transmission of the pilots persists until all the residual pilots in the buffer queue are streamed to the UDP port. Only in this way is data transmission ensured to be conducted without any loss.

Depending on the symbol index, pilot symbols with even indexes are chosen to be transmitted whereas the pilot symbols with odd indexes are discarded. This approach efficiently implements the down-sampling process. Notably, to synchronize different control loops and avoid race conditions, the LabView platform mandates a delay of one millisecond in the loop where each pilot symbol is written to the UDP port. As a result, it takes approximately 100 milliseconds to stream all of the 100 pilot symbols and the resulting data sampling rate is 1 KHz.

4.5 Implementation of the Target-tracking Module

The target-tracking module is supposed to concurrently perform three tasks: reading pilots from a UDP port, tracking human motion, and displaying positioning results. To fulfil these requirements in a software program, the multi-thread programming approach is adopted for a lightweight implementation. Correspondingly, this module comprises three concurrent threads: a pilot-reading thread, a signal-processing thread, and a displaying thread. To clearly explain the operation of this module, a flowchart is illustrated in Figure 4.11. Once the program is started, the three threads are initialized simultaneously by the main process. The functionalities for every thread are introduced below. The pilot-reading thread consistently reads pilot samples from the UDP port

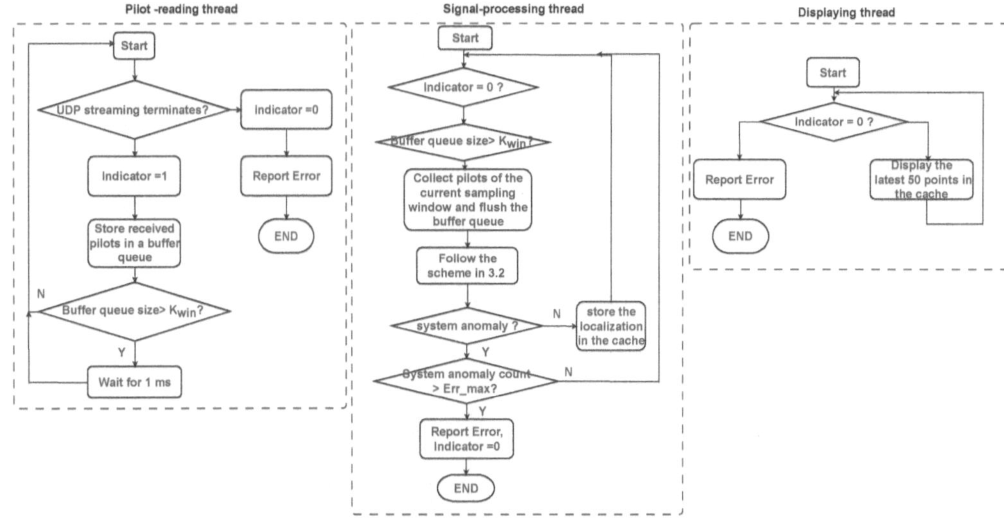

Figure 4.11: Flowchart for the target-tracking module

and temporarily stores them in a buffer queue. Once the pilots' sample size reaches the size of a sampling window, the signal-processing thread imports the pilots from the queue and the queue is flushed for the next sampling window. Concurrently, the signal-processing thread performs target detection and tracking based on the scheme presented in Chapter 3. Once a new positioning estimation is completed, the displaying thread updates the positioning on the monitor. The target-tracking module is developed via Python 3.8 and a screenshot of the localization demonstration is shown in Fig 4.12. It is also worth

Figure 4.12: Screenshot of the localization demonstration

noting that a communication mechanism among threads is also designed to handle exceptions and streamline the entire procedure. On the one hand, once the streaming from the UDP port ceases, whether it be a normal termination of data transmission or a time-out, the pilot-reading thread will detect the occurrence and signal an indicator to terminate the entire program. On the other hand, if the signal-processing thread identifies continuous system anomalies, it will dispatch an indicator to terminate the program.

4.6　Conclusion

This chapter details the implementation of the real-time localization demonstrator. Aligned with the LTE signal structure and comprising a single wireless link, this demonstrator is composed of a customized real-time pilot streaming interface and a concurrent target-tracking module that implements the localization scheme proposed in Chapter 3. Tests have validated that the demonstrator meets the requirement for pilot streaming and signal processing at the data sampling rate of 1 KHz.

Chapter 5

Experimental Evaluations

5.1 Introduction

This chapter presents detailed experimental evaluations of this real-time human motion detection and tracking system, aiming to thoroughly assess the system's localization performance and validate its suitability in diverse scenarios. Section 5.2 provides an overview of the experimental assessment, covering testing methodologies, data processing and visualization methods. Section 5.3 introduces the calibration procedure for the transceiver channels. Section 5.4 presents the impact of UE locations on the localization performance and then determines an optimized UE location for subsequent evaluations. Section 5.5 reveals the impact of walking speed on tracking accuracy. Section 5.6 extends the application of this system to non-line-of-sight (NLoS) scenarios. Section 5.7 concludes the results of the experimental evaluations.

5.2 Overview of the Experimental Evaluations

The experimental evaluations were performed in a lab environment shown in Figure 5.1. This lab environment represents a typical indoor scenario with abundant multi-path signal propagation. Various strong reflectors, including glass windows, wooden desks, concrete walls, and the ground floor etc. surround the transmitter and the receivers. Landmarks are posted on the ground floor to mark one-meter intervals on both axes. Throughout the evaluations, a participant walked along three planned trajectories at various speeds to thoroughly assess the system's real-time tracking performance. Moreover, experiments include both LoS and NLoS scenarios for a comprehensive assessment. To better validate the tracking performance of this system, the impact of the UE location on the tracking accuracy is studied in advance to determine the optimized UE location, defined by the parameter combination $(Dist\_TR, \theta^s)$, with the best localization performance.

Figure 5.1: Evaluation scenario

5.2.1 Hardware Setup and Software Configuration

Figure 5.2 illustrates the experimental hardware setup. The BS employs three receive antennas in a linear array, which is assembled on an antenna mount. The antenna spacing is $D_{01} = 40mm$ and $D_{12} = 42mm$ respectively. On the other hand, the UE utilizes a single transmit antenna at the same height as the BS antennas, located at a distance from the BS antennas. Based on the tests in Section 5.4, the optimized UE location was found to be defined by $(Dist\_TR = 200 \quad cm, \theta^s = -45°)$

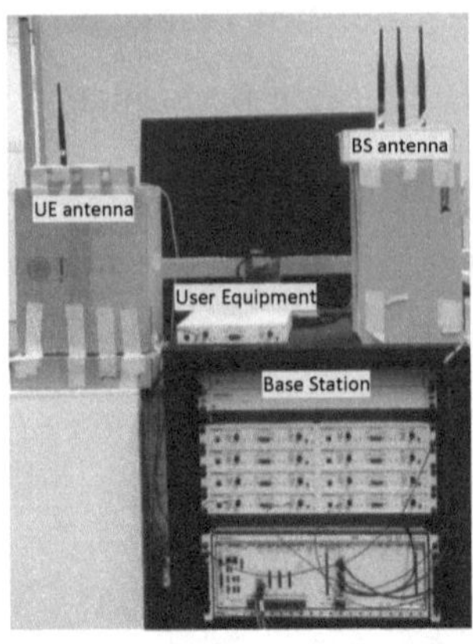

Figure 5.2: Experiment hardware setup

An LTE link is configured with the MAF software on both the BS and the UE controllers. To ensure a stable wireless connection, the transmit power and receive gain for UL and DL links are specifically configured as listed in Table 5.1. The UL link utilizes only one spatial layer (Spatial layer 0) for transmission and the binary symbols are QPSK-modulated. Screenshots for software configuration at the BS and the UE are shown in 5.3. The frame schedule employed in the evaluations is described in Section 4.2 and the consequent data sampling rate is 1KHz. The center frequency is 3.1 GHz and the subcarrier frequencies are specified in (5.1).

$$\begin{cases} f_{sub}^{UL} = 3.1 \pm 7.5 \times 10^{-6} \times N_{ind}^{UL} \quad (GHz) \\ N_{ind}^{UL} : 1, 2, ...600 \end{cases} \tag{5.1}$$

(a) MAF software setup for BS

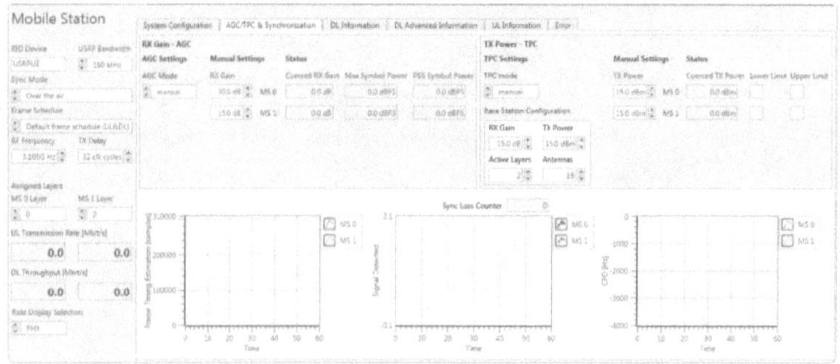

(b) MAF software setup for UE

Figure 5.3: MAF software setup for BS and UE

Table 5.1: Transmitted power and receive gain for the evaluations

	Transmitted Power (dBm)	Receive Gain (dB)
BS	15	30
UE	15	25

5.2.2 Evaluation Methodology

The evaluations aim to comprehensively assess the localization performance
and suitability of this real-time tracking system. A participant walked along
three trajectories illustrated in Figure 5.4 in the assessments. The tracking
performance is assessed by deviations from the theoretical ground truths in
different scenarios.

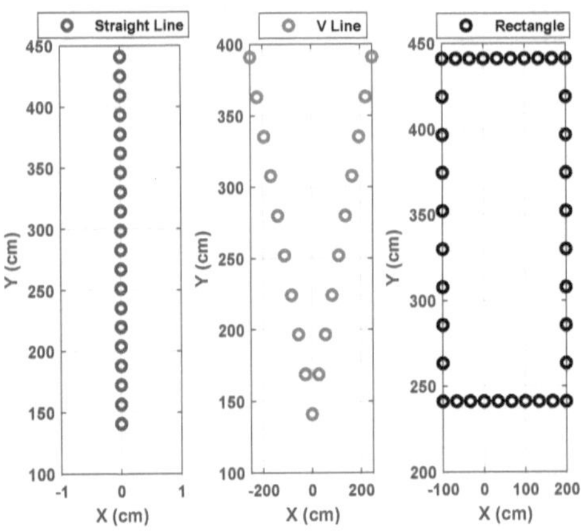

Figure 5.4: Theoretical ground truths

Firstly, the impact of the UE location on the tracking accuracy was thoroughly
investigated to obtain an optimized UE location for the subsequent tests. Experimental studies reveal that both transmitter-to-receiver (TR) distance and
AoA of static LoS signals significantly affect tracking performance.

Secondly, the study examined the impact of walking speed on tracking accuracy.
This was assessed by comparing the tracking accuracy for the V-line trajectory
and the rectangle trajectory when a participant walked at different velocities.

In addition, the application of the system was further extended to NLoS scenarios. Although the signal model assumes a LoS dynamic signal, the system

showcases promising performance in NLoS scenarios. Two cases were tested for the NLoS evaluations, In the first c ase, L oS p ropagation w as obstructed by cardboard boxes. In the second scenario, thick wooden boards were used as barriers. The tracking accuracy in both cases was compared with the LoS benchmark to assess the system's performance in challenging environments.

5.2.3   Data Processing and Visualization Methods

In this book, tracking accuracy is assessed by localization deviations from theoretical ground truths in different s cenarios. W hen a p articipant walked, timing was recorded by a timer application on the mobile phone. The partic-ipant walked at an approximately constant speed in each evaluation and the theoretical motion traces versus time are derived for different s cenarios. More-over, to quantitatively analyze the tracking errors, the cumulative distribution function (CDF) is adopted to analyze the localization deviations. Additionally, 50th percentile and 80th percentile errors are presented to characterize tracking errors.

5.3   Calibration of the Transceiver Channels

According to (3.16), it is necessary to determine $\angle U_{1,m}$, phase difference of CSI components between the 1_{st} antenna and the m_{th} antenna. As the RF channels include the antennas, cables and transceiver channels, an over-the-air calibration procedure is adopted to determine this phase difference between the two antennas. Figure 5.5 illustrates the phase calibration schematic dia-gram and its implementation setup. As is shown in Figure 5.5 (b), due to the time-variant phase of the received signals, the relative phase difference between the m_{th} $(m = 1, 2, 3)$ antenna under test (AUT) and a reference transceiver channel on the same MIMO Framework platform is first measured. Then, the phase difference between 1_{st} antenna and the m_{th} antenna can be derived from (5.2). To measure the phase difference between an antenna and the reference transceiver channel, a power divider is used to split the input from the UE into two outputs. One output is connected to the transmit antenna aligned with one AUT, and the other output is connected to the reference transceiver port. The phase difference between an AUT and the reference transceiver channel is then calculated by (5.2) (a). Following the procedure, the variation of $\angle U_{1,2}$ and $\angle U_{1,3}$ versus frequency are plotted in Figure 5.6. The orange line represents $\angle U_{1,2}$ versus frequency and blue line represents $\angle U_{1,3}$. The phase differences have a linear relationship with frequency because the phases are caused by RF paths of different lengths.

(a) Phase calibration implementation

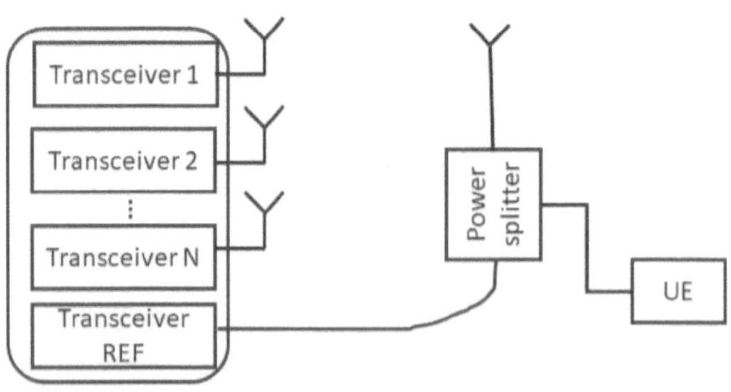

(b) Phase calibration schematics

Figure 5.5: Phase calibration procedure

$$\begin{cases} \angle U_{m,ref} = \angle CSI_{m,ref} & (a) \\ \angle U_{1,m} = \angle U_{1,ref} - \angle U_{m,ref} & (b) \end{cases} \tag{5.2}$$

$\angle U_{m,ref}$: phase difference between the Antenna m and the reference transceiver channel

$\angle CSI_{m,ref}$: cross-correlation of Antenna m and the reference transceiver channel

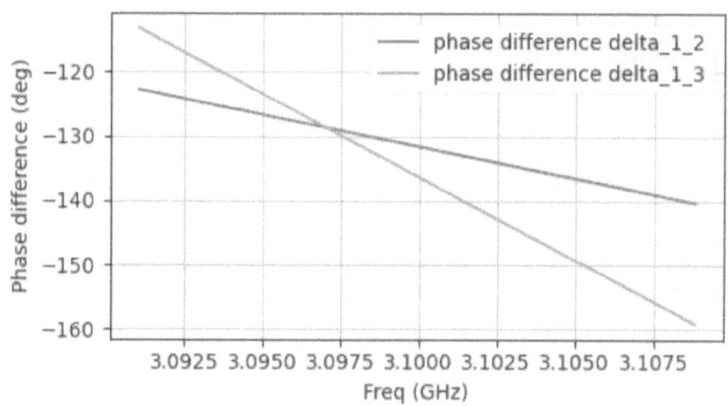

Figure 5.6: Phase difference between the antennas

5.4 Impact of UE Locations on the Tracking Accuracy

The evaluations prove that both the TX-to-RX distance ($Dist\_TR$) and the AoA of static LoS signals (θ^s) substantially affect the localization accuracy. To determine an optimized UE position with the best tracking accuracy for the performance assessments, various UE locations, defined by parameter combinations of ($Dist\_TR, \theta^s$), were examined. Firstly, the effect of AoA was studied while the TX-to-RX distance was kept invariant with $Dist\_TR = 200cm$. Secondly, the effect of TX-to-RX distance was investigated after an optimized AoA had been determined. Consequently, an optimized UE location was determined through this iterative process. To adjust the TX-to-RX distance, the UE was moved throughout the experiments for convenience.

5.4.1 Impact of θ^s on Tracking Accuracy

Localization performance is assessed when $Dist\_TR$ initially keeps 200 cm while θ^s equals $-30°, -45°, -60°, -90°$. Figure 5.7 - Figure 5.9 illustrate the localized trajectories and corresponding CDFs of tracking errors on both the x-axis and y-axis. Table 5.3 lists the 50th and 80th percentile errors. The experimental results manifest that θ^s affects localization deviations considerably. Regarding localization deviations on both axes, UE position at $(Dist\_TR = 200 \quad cm, \theta^s = -45°)$ achieves the best tracking performance in this assessment. Specifically, the 50th and the 80th percentile tracking error along the x-axis are respectively less than 21 cm and 43.8 cm. However, the tracking accuracy degrades to 38 cm for the 50th error and 71 cm for the 80th percentile error in the y-axis direction.

Table 5.2: Localization deviation vs TR_Dist

	Straight line		V line				Rectangle			
TR distance	y axis (cm)		x axis (cm)		y axis (cm)		x axis (cm)		y axis (cm)	
	50%	80%	50%	80%	50%	80%	50%	80%	50%	80%
150	246	318	149	189	294	339	145	196	300	400
200	38	53	21	44	18	52	12	36	24	71
250	90	149	23	43	41	122	35	53	115	168

5.4.2 Impact of $Dist\_TR$ on Tracking Accuracy

To determine the optimized $Dist\_TR$ while θ^s is kept as $-45°$, localization deviations are examined when $Dist\_TR$ respectively equals 150 cm, 200 cm and 300 cm . Both the localized trajectories and corresponding CDFs for these UE positions are depicted in Figure 5.10 - Figure 5.12. Table 5.2 lists the 50th

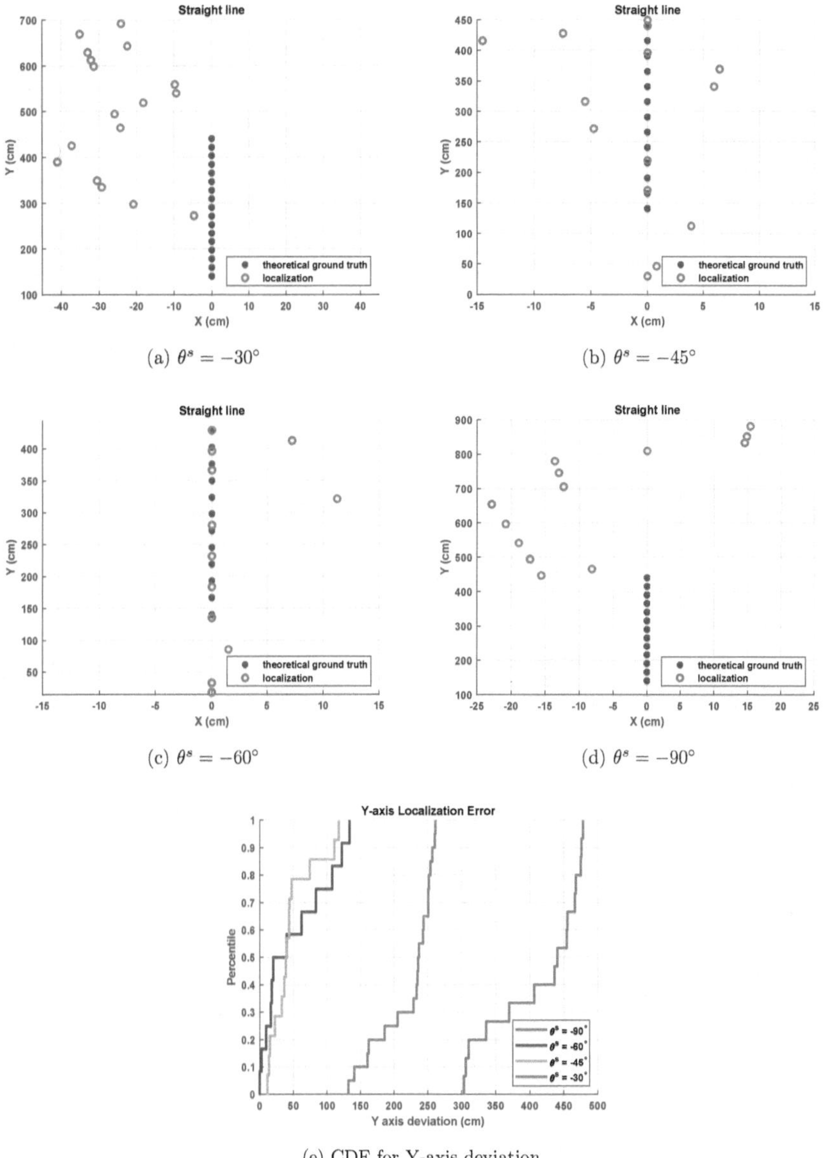

(a) $\theta^s = -30°$

(b) $\theta^s = -45°$

(c) $\theta^s = -60°$

(d) $\theta^s = -90°$

(e) CDF for Y-axis deviation

Figure 5.7: Straight line: $Dist\_TR = 200 \quad (cm)$

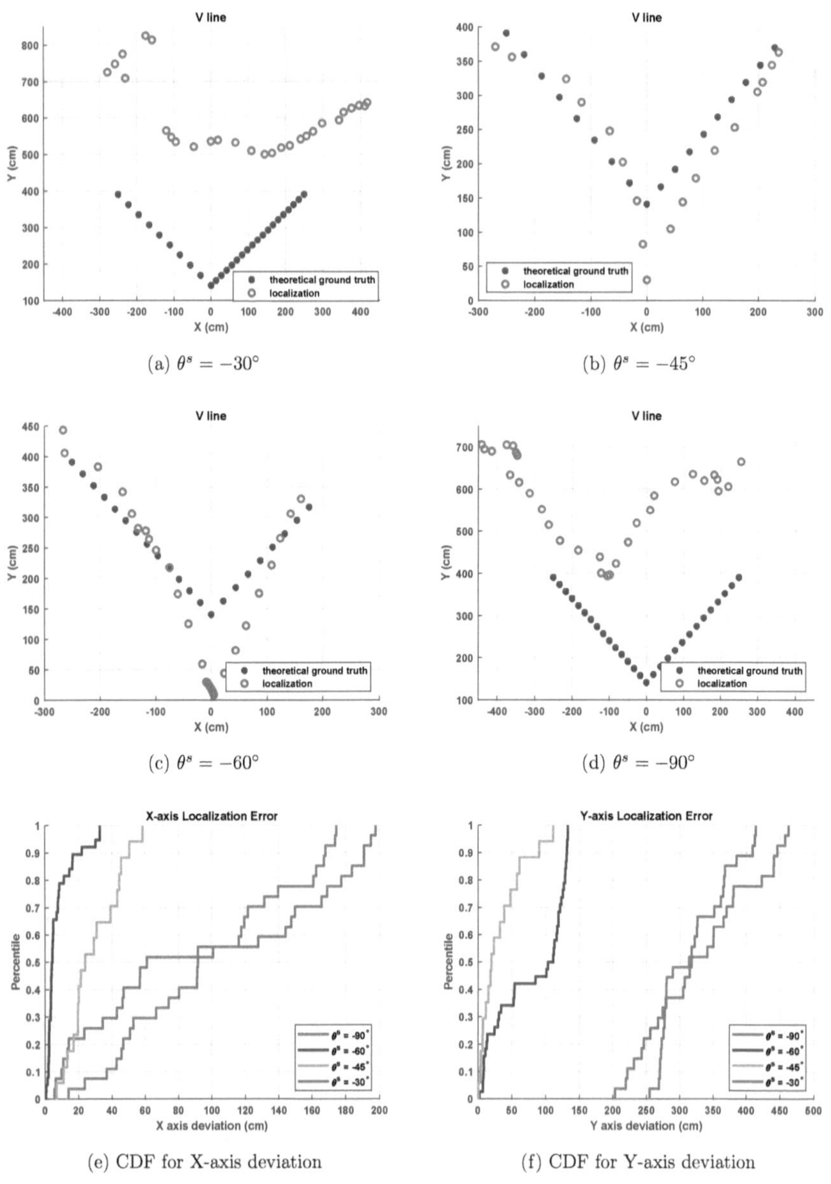

(a) $\theta^s = -30°$

(b) $\theta^s = -45°$

(c) $\theta^s = -60°$

(d) $\theta^s = -90°$

(e) CDF for X-axis deviation

(f) CDF for Y-axis deviation

Figure 5.8: V-line : $Dist\_TR = 200(cm)$

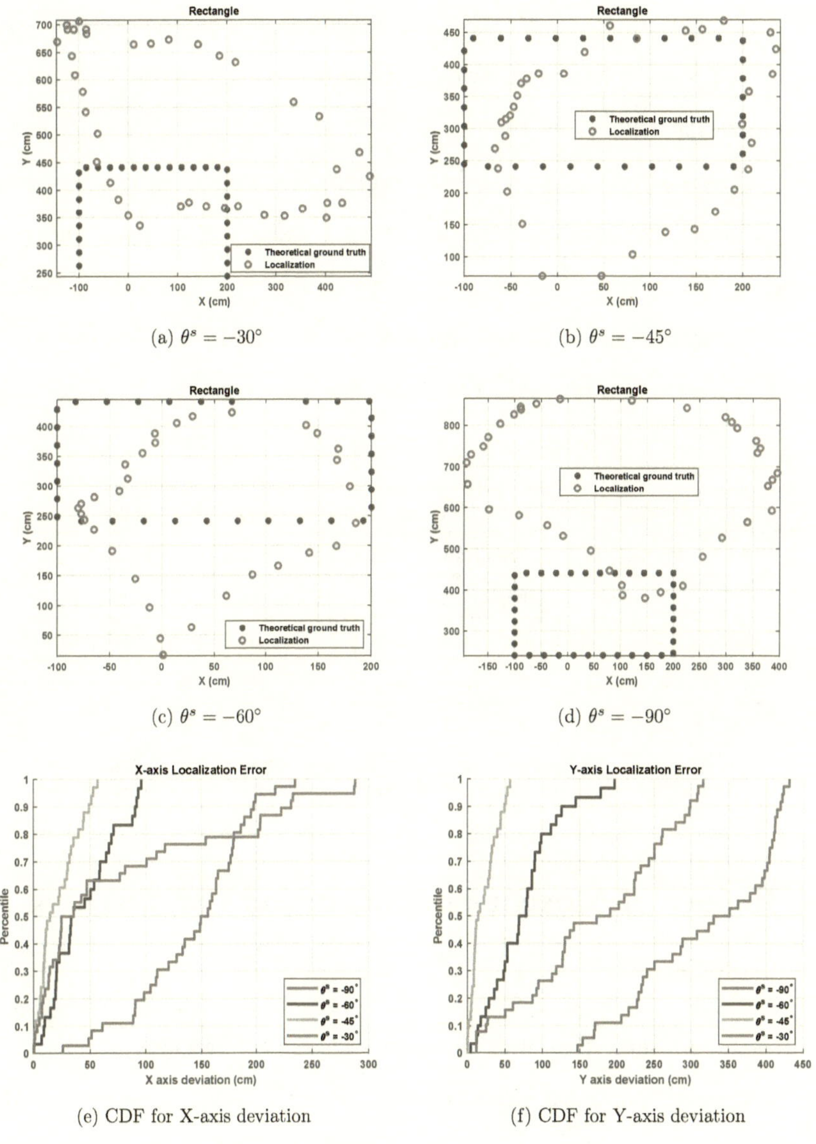

(a) $\theta^s = -30°$

(b) $\theta^s = -45°$

(c) $\theta^s = -60°$

(d) $\theta^s = -90°$

(e) CDF for X-axis deviation

(f) CDF for Y-axis deviation

Figure 5.9: Rectangle : $Dist\_TR = 200(cm)$

percentile and 80th percentile errors. It is clearly shown that among the various UE locations under test, the best tracking performance is witnessed at $(Dist\_TR = 200\ cm, \theta^s = -45°)$. Hence, this location is chosen as an opti-mized UE position for the subsequent evaluations in this book. Besides, it is also noted that localization deviations rise when the human target moves closer to the receiver. This is attributed to a substantial amplification of the dynamic signal's intensity, which approaches that of the LoS static signal when the per-son approaches the receiver. Consequently, the accuracy of the approximation in (3.13) to separate dynamic from static components diminishes, compared to the scenarios when a target moves farther away from the receiver.

Table 5.3: Localization deviation vs θ^s

$\theta^s(deg)$	Straight line		V line				Rectangle			
	y axis (cm)		x axis (cm)		y axis (cm)		x axis (cm)		y axis (cm)	
	50%	80%	50%	80%	50%	80%	50%	80%	50%	80%
-30	235	252	91	147.8	290	399	26	163	158	260
-45	38	53	21	43.8	18	52	12	36	24	71
-60	20	99	4	8.6	110	130	29	69	76	112
-90	438	468	57	172	314	365	148	180	328	408

5.5 Impact of Movement Velocity on the Tracking Accuracy

The assessments show that walking speeds also affect tracking accuracy. The evaluations were conducted three times each or the V-line trajectory and the rectangle trajectory, when a participant walked at different velocities. The walking velocities were approximately 0.7 m/s, 1 m/s and 1.2 m/s and are respectively labelled as "slow", "medium" and "fast". Figure 5.13 illustrates the

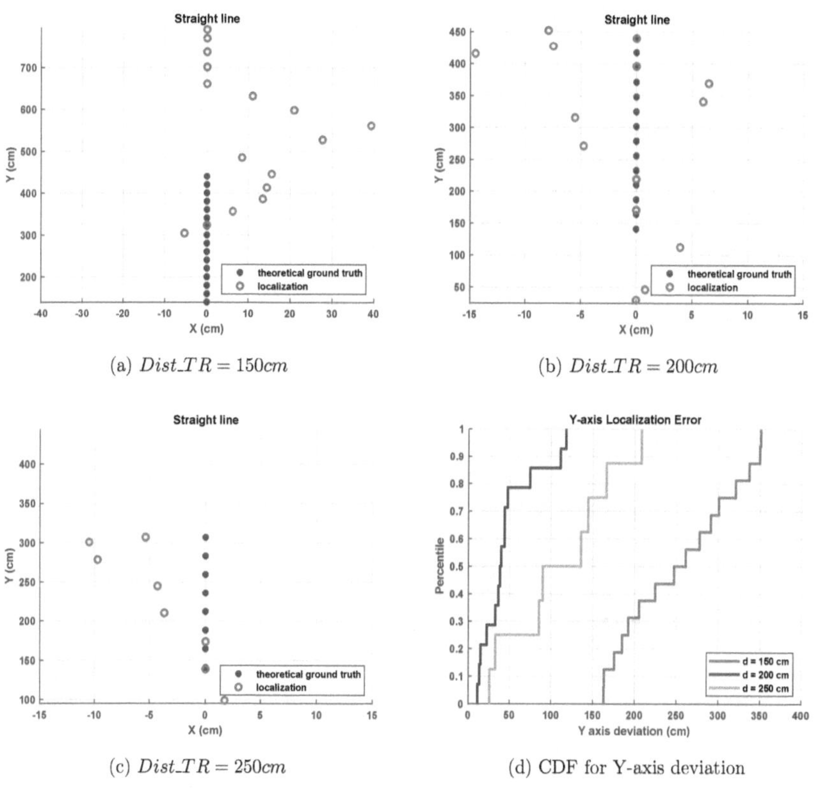

(a) $Dist\_TR = 150cm$

(b) $Dist\_TR = 200cm$

(c) $Dist\_TR = 250cm$

(d) CDF for Y-axis deviation

Figure 5.10: Straight line : $\theta^s = -45°$

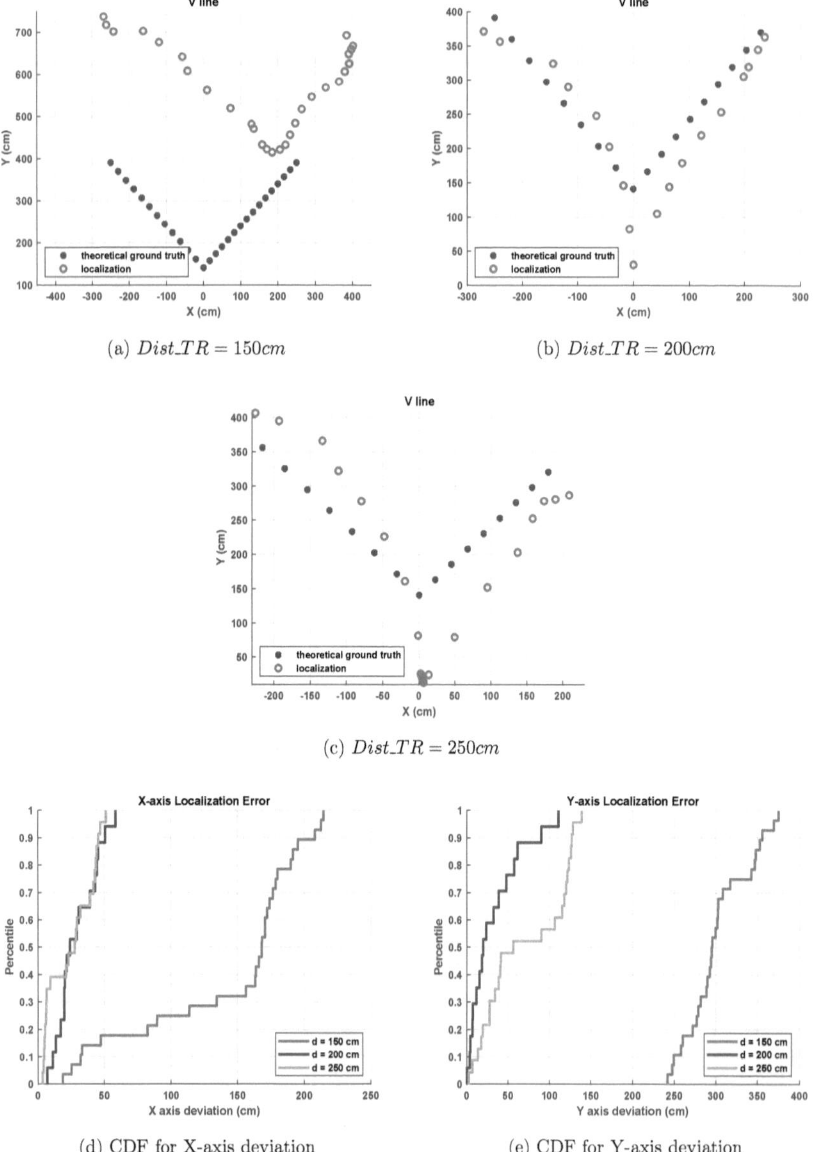

(a) $Dist\_TR = 150cm$

(b) $Dist\_TR = 200cm$

(c) $Dist\_TR = 250cm$

(d) CDF for X-axis deviation

(e) CDF for Y-axis deviation

Figure 5.11: V-line : $\theta^s = -45°$

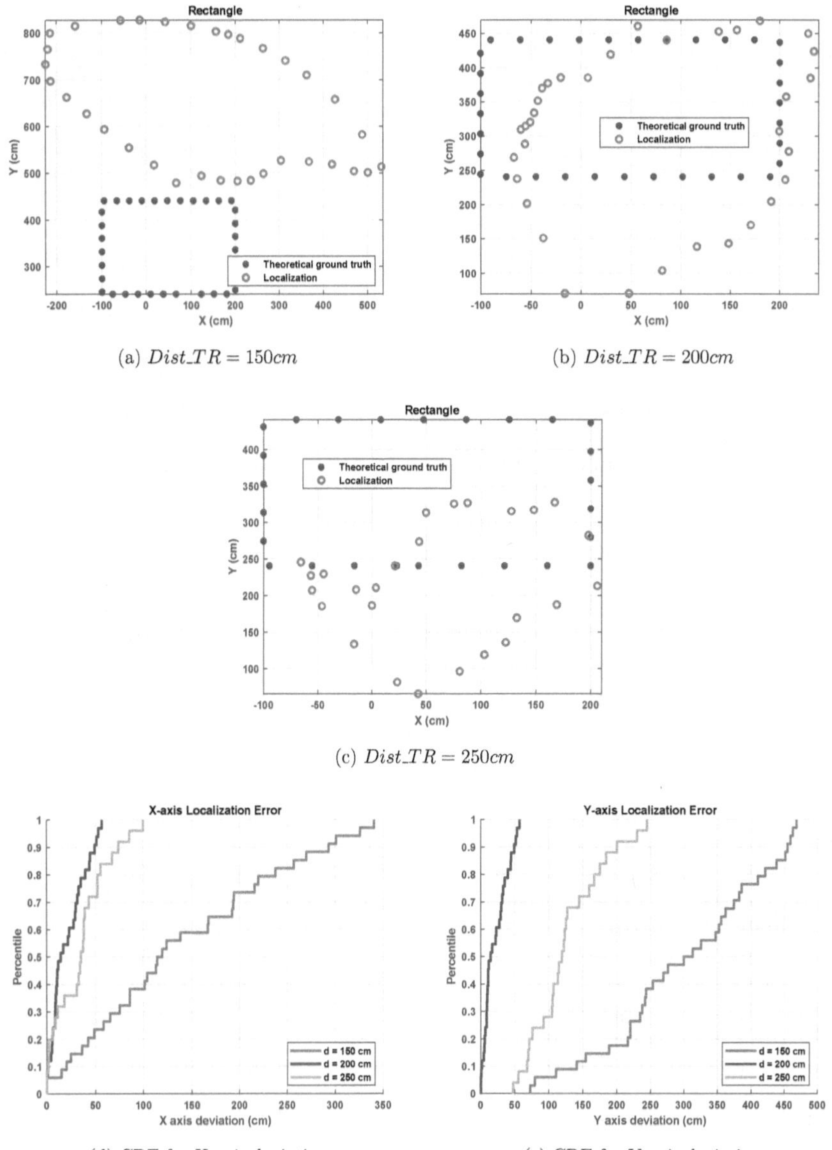

(a) $Dist\_TR = 150cm$ (b) $Dist\_TR = 200cm$

(c) $Dist\_TR = 250cm$

(d) CDF for X-axis deviation   (e) CDF for Y-axis deviation

Figure 5.12: Rectangle : $\theta^s = -45°$

localized path and the CDFs for the V-line trajectory. The 50% and 80% errors are listed in Table 5.4. It demonstrates that the test with the "medium" speed achieves the minimum tracking errors for the V-line trajectory and the "fast" speed results in similar deviations. By contrast, the deviations rise notably with the "slow" speed. Likewise, Figure 5.14 depicts the corresponding results for the rectangle trajectory tracking. The 50% and 80% deviations are presented in Table 5.4. It is shown that the "medium" speed leads to the best tracking performance, whereas the "slow" speed results in the poorest tracking performance among the test results. By analyzing the above test results, it can be concluded that if a person moves very slowly, statistical localization errors tend to accumulate due to increased exposure to areas with low tracking accuracy.

Table 5.4: Localization deviation vs different speeds

speed	V line				Rectangle			
	x axis (cm)		y axis (cm)		x axis (cm)		y axis (cm)	
	50%	80%	50%	80%	50%	80%	50%	80%
fast	11	55	30	68	32	55	52	87
medium	21	44	18	52	12	36	24	71
slow	65	21	101	125	36	46	36	105

5.6 Evaluations in Non-Light-of-Sight Scenarios

The evaluations in non-light-of-sight (NLoS) scenarios were performed in two cases, as shown in Figure 5.15. In the first case, empty cardboard boxes of 3 millimetres in thickness obstructed the signal's LoS propagation between the UE and the BS. In this situation, the S-band radio wave can penetrate the boxes through refraction while the LoS signal slightly changes its propagation direction. In the second case, thick wooden boards of 8 cm in thickness were

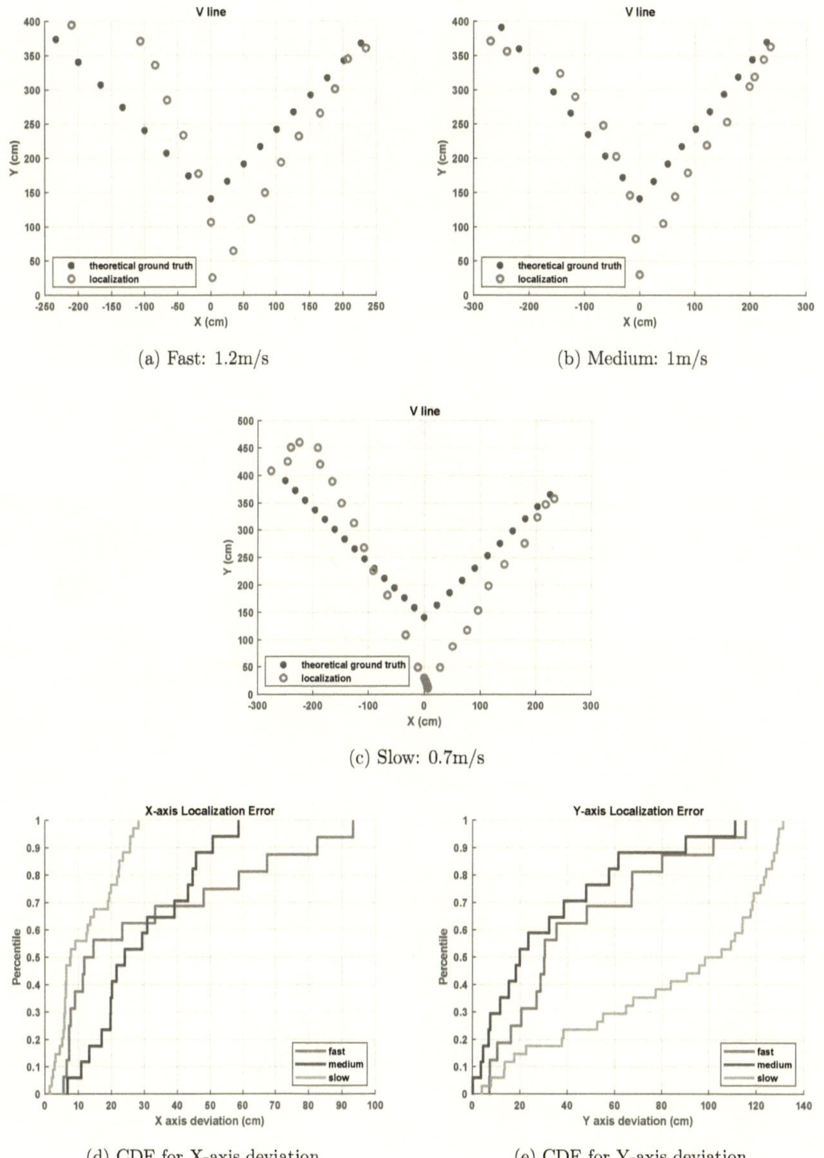

(a) Fast: 1.2m/s

(b) Medium: 1m/s

(c) Slow: 0.7m/s

(d) CDF for X-axis deviation

(e) CDF for Y-axis deviation

Figure 5.13: V-line trajectory tracking with different walking speed

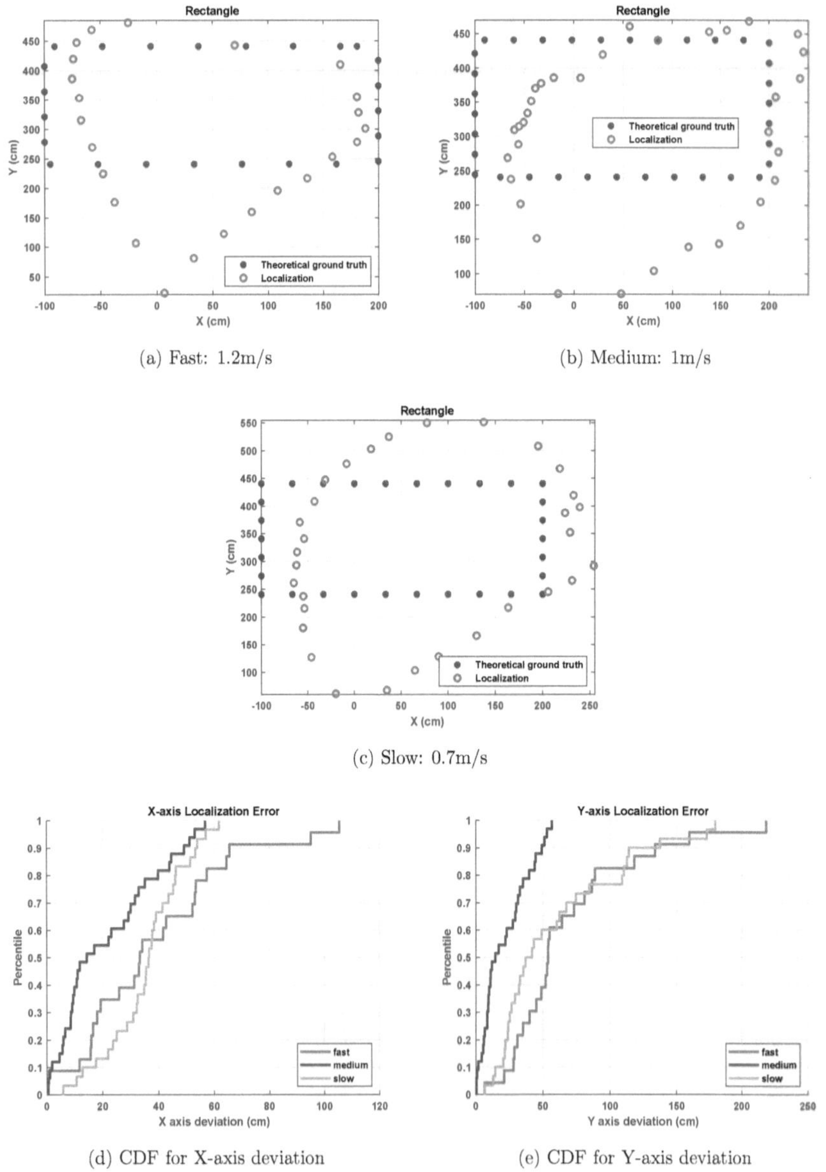

(a) Fast: 1.2m/s

(b) Medium: 1m/s

(c) Slow: 0.7m/s

(d) CDF for X-axis deviation

(e) CDF for Y-axis deviation

Figure 5.14: Rectangle trajectory tracking with different walking speed

placed between the UE and the BS. More multi-path propagation would occur due to scattering when radio waves impinge upon the wooden boards. Localization performance is evaluated for the V-line and rectangle trajectories in both scenarios and was compared with the LoS benchmark.

Figure 5.16 and Figure 5.17 depict respectively the localized paths and CDFs for the V-line trajectory and the rectangle trajectory. As expected, tracking accuracy degrades in both NLoS cases, compared with the LoS case. Specifically, the wooden board case results in larger tracking errors than the cardboard case. In the V-line trajectory assessment, the cardboard scenario results in an 80th percentile error of 86 cm and the wooden board scenario results in an 80th percentile error of 118 cm. Similarly, in the rectangle trajectory assessment, the cardboard scenario witnesses an 80th percentile error of 117 cm and the wooden board scenario witnesses an 80th percentile error of 105 cm. More detailed results are presented in Table 5.5.

Table 5.5: Localization deviation for NLoS scenarios

| | V line | | | | Rectangle | | | |
| | x axis (cm) | | y axis (cm) | | x axis (cm) | | y axis (cm) | |
	50%	80%	50%	80%	50%	80%	50%	80%
LoS	21	44	18	52	12	36	24	71
cardboard	8	15	47	86	22	79	60	117
wooden board	26	34	36	118	24	60	35	105

(a) Cardboard box case   (b) Wooden board case

Figure 5.15: NLoS scenario evaluations

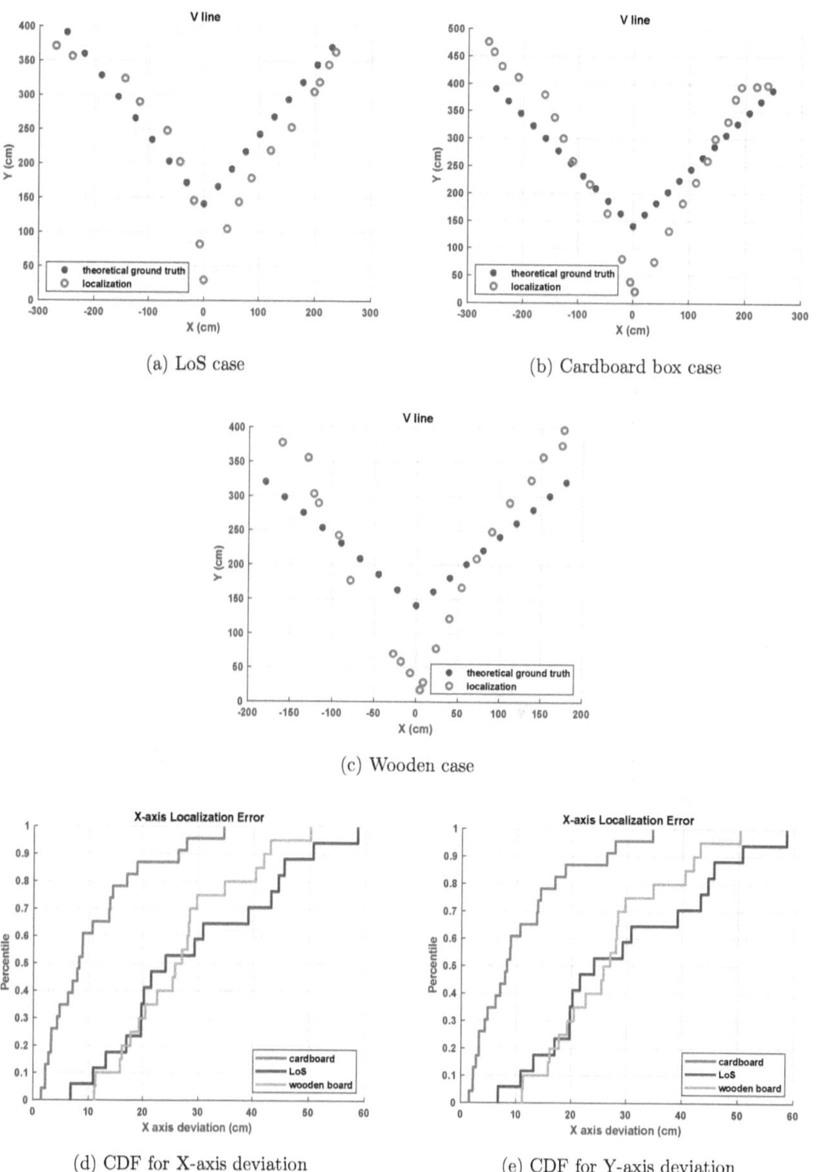

(a) LoS case

(b) Cardboard box case

(c) Wooden case

(d) CDF for X-axis deviation

(e) CDF for Y-axis deviation

Figure 5.16: V-line trajectory tracking in NLoS scenarios

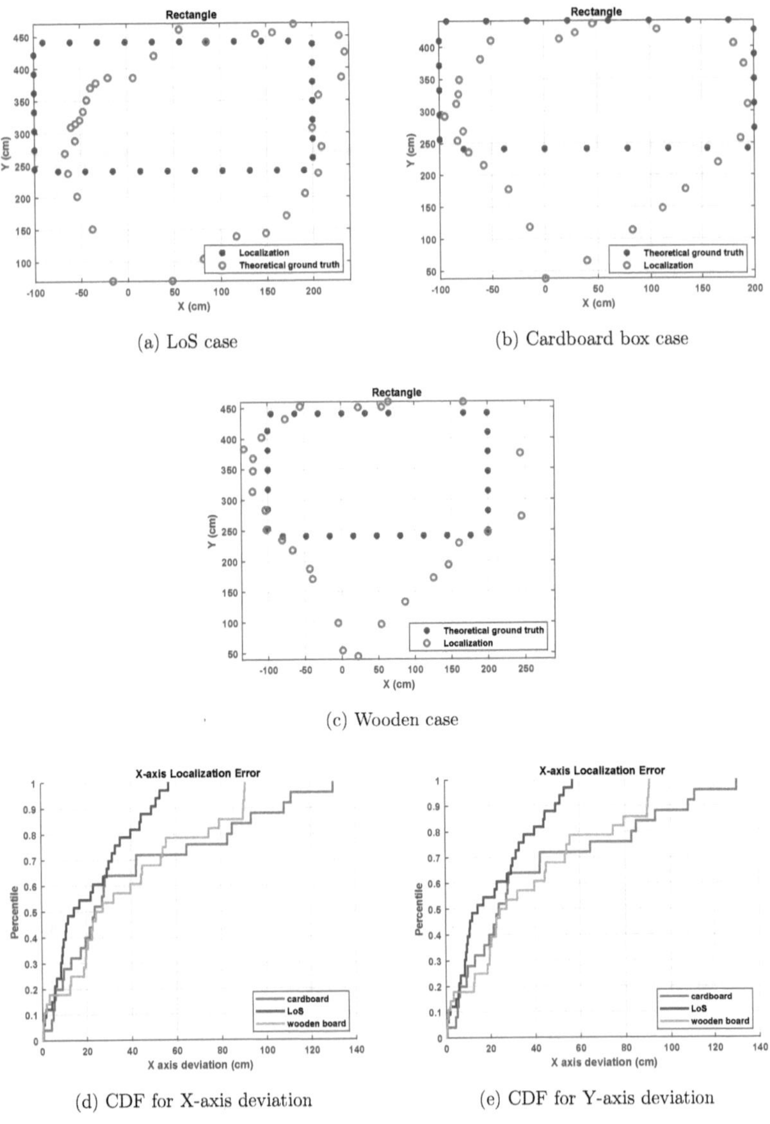

(a) LoS case

(b) Cardboard box case

(c) Wooden case

(d) CDF for X-axis deviation

(e) CDF for Y-axis deviation

Figure 5.17: Rectangle trajectory tracking in NLoS scenarios

5.7   Conclusion

This chapter presents detailed evaluations of the localization performance of this human motion tracking system. Experimental studies demonstrate that when the UE is located at $(Dist\_TR = 200 \quad cm, \theta^s = -45°)$, this system enables the best tracking accuracy with sub-meter precision. Furthermore, it is discovered that the target's walking speed influences localization deviations. Furthermore, the extension to NLoS scenarios is also evaluated and the demonstrator shows the capability to track the target with slightly larger positioning errors than in LoS scenarios.

Chapter 6

Conclusions and Future Work

In this book, we have successfully designed and implemented a human motion detection and localization demonstrator using LTE-based uplink pilots. It enables real-time tracking of moving human targets. This chapter reviews the main contributions of the book and looks forward to our future work.

6.1   Summary of Outcomes

In Chapter 3, a well-structured human motion detection and tracking scheme is detailed. This scheme comprises a robust human motion detection mechanism that relies on the median phase standard deviation (MPSTD) of CSI ratio samples as a motion detection indicator (MDI). To confirm genuine human motion and mitigate false detection, this mechanism follows an iterative procedure, combining the MDI specifications and Doppler frequency estimates in a joint window. The localization scheme incorporates a CSIR-based Doppler estimator and the maximum likelihood estimation-based (MLE-based) AoA and delay estimators, enabling effective and accurate human localization with low computational complexity. The experimental evaluations in Chapter 5 validate that the proposed scheme enables sub-meter positioning accuracy with real-time performance.

Chapter 4 details the design and implementation of this demonstration system. Built on the NI Massive MIMO prototyping test bed, this system comprises a

customized real-time pilot-streaming interface and a real-time target-tracking
module. The pilot-streaming interface is capable of handling massive LTE-
based pilots in a MIMO setup, while the real-time target-tracking module concurrently performs three tasks: reading pilots, tracking human motion, as well
as displaying positioning results.

6.2 Future Work

This research work can be extended in the following two aspects.

First, experimental evaluations reveal that the localization precision deterio-
rates when the target approaches the receive antennas. In particular, when the
target walks within 2 meters of the receiver antennas, the positioning deviations
substantially rise. This phenomenon can be primarily attributed to the under-
lying model assumption that the static component significantly outweighs the
LoS dynamic component in a snapshot. Following this proposition, the static
component is approximated by the arithmetic means of the CFR power in a
sampling window. However, this approximation becomes less reliable as the
LoS dynamic component increases rapidly when the human target moves to-
ward the receiver antennas. Therefore, the method needs to be improved in
this specific situation.

Second, the demonstrator fails to undertake multi-target recognition and positioning, a crucial requirement in many applications. Given that the real-time
positioning of multi-targets via a single wireless link remains an open research
problem, there still exist various challenges. A potential solution is to discriminate different echo sources by leveraging the signal features across multiple
signal domains based on the spatial sparsity of the targets. This specifies the
target of our future work.